SINGAPORE'S REAL ESTATE SECRETS

HOW TO CREATE WEALTH & ACHIEVE FINANCIAL FREEDOM WITH PROVEN INVESTING STRATEGIES

CEEKAY

PARTRIDGE

Copyright © 2022 by CEEKAY.

ISBN: Hardcover   978-1-5437-7210-4
       Softcover   978-1-5437-7208-1
       eBook   978-1-5437-7209-8

All rights reserved. No part of this book may be used or reproduced by any means, graphic, electronic, or mechanical, including photocopying, recording, taping or by any information storage retrieval system without the written permission of the author except in the case of brief quotations embodied in critical articles and reviews.

Because of the dynamic nature of the Internet, any web addresses or links contained in this book may have changed since publication and may no longer be valid. The views expressed in this work are solely those of the author and do not necessarily reflect the views of the publisher, and the publisher hereby disclaims any responsibility for them.

Print information available on the last page.

To order additional copies of this book, contact
Toll Free +65 3165 7531 (Singapore)
Toll Free +60 3 3099 4412 (Malaysia)
orders.singapore@partridgepublishing.com

www.partridgepublishing.com/singapore

To Jesus, thank you for blessing me with the wisdom and knowledge to write this book.

To my dearest family, especially my father who brought me up almost single-handedly.

And my amazing grandmother, aunt for loving me so deeply, and my step-mother for treating me like her very own.

To my loving partner Noelle – your love, devotion and support are the true wealth of my life.

To my Sifu Dan Lok, thank you for seeing the potential in me and guiding me along the way not just about business, but also about life.

Also, thank you EdgeProp for the amazing data and analytical tools that have helped me greatly for all these years with my real estate research work. Without EdgeProp's data sources, this book wouldn't be as complete as it should be.

CONTENTS

Introduction ix

Chapter 1: You're Born To Be Rich 1

- Secret #1 – Inside The Mind Of A Successful Investor 3
- Secret #2 – Top 5 Poor Habits That Hold You Back
  From Riches 8
- Secret #3 – The Friendly Housing Advice You Should
  Never Take 17
- Secret #4 – The Little-Known Truths About Wealth Attraction 22

Chapter 2: Singapore, The Real Estate Gold Mine 27

- Secret #5 – Limited Land, Unlimited Wealth 29
- Secret #6 – Why The Rich Loves The Government 32
- Secret #7 – What You Read Is Not Always Real 36
- Secret #8 – The Path To Gold Is Hidden In Plain Sight 39

Chapter 3: Clarity, Certainty, Confidence 45

- Secret #9 – The 3 Cs Every Investor Needs 47
- Secret #10 – No One's Blowing Property Bubbles 59
- Secret #11 – Most Investors Regret Not Knowing
  This Sooner! 64

Chapter 4: We Need To Talk About Money 69

- Secret #12 – Need More Money? Get It For Free 71
- Secret #13 – Your CPF Money Is Not Always Yours 76
- Secret #14 – How Smart Investors Don't Use Their Own
  Money To Be Rich 81

Chapter 5: Top 5 Costly Mistakes Most Make Unknowingly 87

- Secret #15 - The Ugly Truth About Public Housing 89
- Secret #16 – Why Buying Great Locations Don't Always Work 94
- Secret #17 - Buying Cheap Doesn't Make You Wealthier 106
- Secret #18 - The Greatest Lies Realtors Tell You About Freehold 115
- Secret #19 - The Little Dirty Secrets Developers Didn't Tell You 125

Chapter 6: Where The Money is and The Top 5 Fastest Ways to Get It 133

- Secret #20 - The Simple Way To Earn More While Spending Less 135
- Secret #21 - Big Ways To Big Profits 139
- Secret #22 - Know What The Rich Really Wants 142
- Secret #23 - The Evergreen Demand You Can Always Rely On 147
- Secret #24 - The Reverse Psychology Method That Worked Wonders 150

Chapter 7: You Ain't Successful Till You Sell 155

- Secret #25 - To Hold Or Not To Hold… That's The Question 157
- Secret #26 - Want To Sell With More Profits? STOP Doing This 160
- Secret #27 - The Hidden Lies That Realtors Don't Tell You 163

Chapter 8: Your Multi-Million Legacy Begins 169

- Secret #28 - Your Decision Today Determines Your Children's Future 171
- Secret #29 - Your Million-Dollar Retirement Blueprint 174

Chapter 9: The Final Advice For You, The Next Top Investor 181

- Secret #30 - Top Investors Focus On This More Than R.O.I 183
- Secret #31 - The Art Of Taking Action For Real 187

INTRODUCTION

I have no idea why you're reading this book.

Perhaps you stumbled upon this book by chance. Maybe someone recommended this book to you… Or maybe you are one of my followers on social media. Or perhaps, you just thought that I looked handsome on the book cover…

Kidding.

But one thing that I know, something deep inside you knows that you want more.

More money, more time, more happiness.

You're probably wondering why you are stuck in a rat race of sorts, and why you can't seem to enjoy life more. Perhaps, you are filled with fear and uncertainty over what the world will become, as cost of living continues to escalate and pretty much everything (especially housing) gets more expensive as time passes.

You see, not many people are that interested in changing their lives for the better. In fact, the majority of them tend to lament and complain about their lives, their jobs, their families even… and yet they don't do anything about it. Most people just simply accept life as it is because they feel stuck and powerless.

And I believe YOU ARE DIFFERENT. In a good way.

You have the desire to change your life, to succeed in what you do, and to provide more for your loved ones than what you're doing now.

And this is why I want to congratulate you, because by reading this book, you have already taken that first step out towards a better future for yourself.

In this world, about 97% of the population remains poor. Not just in terms of finances, but also in their mindset towards wealth and money.

And I believe you're going to be among the Top 3% who chooses to live life differently.

Now, you might be thinking, what does this have to do with my book that is about Singapore's Real Estate?

You see, this book isn't just about real estate. I believe that in order to be a truly successful property investor, you need to see things differently from others. That includes your mindset towards wealth, money, and how it is possible to lead a carefree life together with your loved ones without any financial stress.

I hope that this book will not only give you a new perspective but more importantly, a clear way to take action so that you can achieve much more in life than the majority of the population.

However, I don't promise that this book has every answer you need. The truth is, real estate investment is such a diverse topic and there is a lot of contradicting information that confuses most minds. And my mission with this book is to provide you with as much clarity and certainty as possible, so that you can proceed to invest with full confidence.

Before you proceed further with this book, do remember to do your due diligence when it comes to financing your investments, including the latest tax rates, stamp duties, loan interest rates, and more… because I'm not going to go through the detailed technicalities within this book.

There will be a total of 31 Secrets about Singapore's Real Estate (33 actually, if you unlock the bonus chapters online – flip to the last few pages of this book to gain your private access) – but it does not mean that you must implement 100% of everything you read in this book to be a successful real estate investor.

In fact, there will be information that I share that you may or may not agree with, and that's perfectly okay. Everything shared in this book comes purely from my years of experience of studying the market and helping investors for more than 8 years as of now. You may hear different opinions and knowledge from others, and that is still your personal responsibility to figure out what to do with the information you learn.

Absorb what you feel is useful from this book, discard what you disagree with, and it will be best if what you learn helps you to form your own opinion and views when it comes to investing real estate in Singapore.

I don't claim that my opinion is the best, but having managed more than $100 million worth of property investments in my career, I believe my knowledge and insights should help you in one way or another.

So why did I decide to write this book?

To explain that, let me first share what got me into real estate to begin with:

Back in early 2015, I left my previous job as a full-time regular serviceman for the Republic of Singapore Navy, after spending almost 6 years in what most calls it an "iron rice-bowl job" in Chinese (which means 100% job security – it's near impossible to get sacked being in the armed forces).

Interestingly, back in the Navy I assisted to manage Naval Officers' study sponsorships, as well as to handle Mid-Careerists' recruitment packages to bring them back into the force – which also meant that I was entrusted with the Singapore government's money.

I managed millions of taxpayers' money every month – a huge responsibility for me as every single cent spent had to be audited and accounted for. But little did I know back then that this precious experience would prepare me to eventually manage property investors' money today.

Prior to leaving the Navy, I was absolutely clueless as to what my next career choice would be. All I knew was that I wanted to scale my income on my own terms... I wasn't satisfied with a meagre salary of less than $4,000 monthly that I was drawing back then from the armed forces, and there was that inner voice that told me "you deserve to achieve much more than this".

What happened next was just like a God-sent miracle.

It was in late 2014. While on a work trip with my Navy comrades, I coincidentally bumped into an old friend named Danny along the way. In a quick and brief catch up, Danny recommended me to consider joining the real estate industry – and I was taken aback.

Real Estate?! Like... Being a realtor?

I was stumped, but intrigued at the same time.

Frankly, the thought of being a realtor never crossed my mind before. Selling houses? With no basic salary, and purely relying on sales commission for a living? What a complete opposite to my job as a Navy regular serviceman!

Yet I thought to myself – sooner or later I would need to buy my own property anyway, so why not pick up some essential knowledge for my own investments in the future?

So I went ahead to register for the real estate salesperson course, much to the dismay (and violent objections) from my family and peers.

For those who recall, 2014 – 2015 were not great times for the real estate market in Singapore. Most developers and realtors were still reeling from the huge impact caused by major cooling measures implemented by the government in 2013, and plenty of realtors couldn't survive in those trying times. Property prices went down for 3 years straight and confidence in the market was extremely low.

In such circumstances, most people would find it foolish to jump into the real estate industry in those testing times... But I was not one of them.

Well, since young I've been quite different from others. I was the kid who didn't follow the conventional rules. I always believed that fortune favours the brave, so if people told me that joining the real estate industry was a stupid idea, then all the more I would jump right in!

Eventually I went against my parents' objections to tender my resignation from the Navy, even BEFORE I took the real estate examinations. Talk about a huge leap of faith!

Thankfully, by God's grace, I passed the notoriously-difficult real estate examinations in my first attempt, and I have never looked back ever since.

Over the years, my passion and thirst for investment knowledge kept me going. With every property buyer I met, and every developer I worked closely with, I learnt more and more each day on how real estate investments could generate not just lifetime wealth for an individual, but also multi-generational wealth that could feed generations to come.

That's why I decided to write this book, to educate people like you who want to gain access to the same knowledge for yourself.

The sad truth is this - many Singaporeans think that just because they are well-educated, they can easily figure out how property investment works. Like, how difficult could it be, right?

Unfortunately, that's where these people get their hands burnt.

Retirement savings were lost. Hard-earned savings gone.

In a country where almost all citizens receive formal education, it was alarming for me to witness how most of them lacked fundamental knowledge about property investments that resulted in financial distress for them – and I hope that with this book, you will be able to avoid making costly mistakes for your own investments.

This book contains wisdom and knowledge collated through years of research about the real estate market, and also through personal experience gained from working with many property investors.

Beware though, the secrets contained in this book could possibly turn your world upside down in many ways, for there are plenty of insider knowledge that I'm about to share with you... while some of the insights you'll learn might liberate you, there could also be some logic-defying truths that you may struggle to believe.

So you've been warned.

Now if you're ready, let's flip on to the next page to start your journey with me in uncovering Singapore's Real Estate Secrets...

CHAPTER 1

YOU'RE BORN TO BE RICH

It is your destiny to enjoy a carefree, fulfilling life without any stress and worries about your finances...

Secret #1 – Inside The Mind Of A Successful Investor

"Whatever the mind of man can conceive and believe, it can achieve." – Napoleon Hill

Real estate investments have been around a long time. It has created wealth for many, but also destroyed the lives of many.

There are those who could leave behind a multi-million legacy for their future generations; there's also those who continue to be stuck in the poverty cycle, unable to retire comfortably as most of their hard-earned savings went towards maintaining a shelter over their heads.

What sets a successful investor apart from others?

Is it just knowledge? Or perhaps they had insider tips that others don't?

Is it because the rich simply had more money to spend, therefore being able to generate more profits than the poor?

Well, I cannot give you a definite answer on the above... But what I am certain about is that success for any property investor starts with the mind first - the way you think will determine the results you get.

Before a painter completes a masterpiece, he sees the whole artwork in his mind first.

Before a musician plays a song, he hears the whole tune in his mind first.

Think about every bit of technology we have today – be it from your mobile phone, computer, the television and so on... the technology exists because someone first imagined the possibility before achieving the technological breakthrough.

The power of the mind has always served mankind throughout history, and countless inventions relied on the imaginations of the inventors to turn vision into reality. That is exactly the kind of power that already exists in your mind – it's just that you have yet to tap on the vast potential that's within you.

It is totally possible for you to create the life that you want, and generate the wealth that you want, without having to go through unnecessary pains and stress.

To make it easier for you, here are 3 things that you can focus on to set yourself on the path of success:

1. **DESIRE – I WANT IT THEREFORE I'LL GET IT**

    Before you can enjoy any success, you need to first WANT IT.

    Now this may sound like a no-brainer, but there are indeed people who do not dare to want a better life.

    To these people, having a better life means more financial stress and burdens – they are afraid that having more money means higher expenses, and therefore higher risks of losing it all if they get retrenched from their job in times of recession.

    Guess what they tend to say?

    "It's okay, I am easily content"... "I don't need to stay in such a nice house, I don't need to drive a nice car"... "I am not greedy, what I have now is more than enough for me".

    While there's nothing wrong in being truly content, there are also hypocrites who refuse to admit that deep inside them, a good life is what they really want.

    Just look at those who go for staycations in hotels... or those who visit posh restaurants once in a while with their family and friends. Then there's those who change their mobile phones to the latest models once every 2 years while re-contracting with the telcos... The list goes on.

    The truth is – they all want a good life. And that's perfectly okay – what isn't okay is to DENY that they want it. That denial is exactly what limits them to enjoying life just once in a while!

    If a better life is what you want, then boldly claim and declare it!

Imagine this – think about the dream house that you want to stay in. How big would it be? How many people would be staying together? Where would the location of the house be?

Think about your dream holiday destination too. Which country and city would it be? Who would you bring along with you, and where would be the places you would like to visit?

When you imagine and visualise all these things of your desires, doesn't it fill you with joy and happiness? These good feelings you felt aren't hallucinations – it's real. This is however just a small sample size of the happiness you can get – imagine the full scale of your happiness when you finally achieve your goals!

I know there's that fire in you, waiting to be ignited, so that you can live the life of your dreams...

So light up that fire now, and keep it burning.

2. **BELIEF – I AM CERTAIN THAT I'LL GET IT!**

Now that you have a desire to change your life, the next crucial step is to believe.

This is the step where most people fail, simply because they are unable to overcome their fears, worries, and even their own ego. As a result, no matter how strong their desire was in the beginning, the fire within just wouldn't last for long.

Some people even have difficulties believing that it is possible to lead a carefree life, because they witnessed their parents' struggles and it left a deep impression in their subconscious mind that making money is always difficult.

It is especially so in Asian culture, where we often heard our elders say "don't waste your hard-earned money". That was exactly the kind of thoughts planted into our minds from young – earning money was always perceived to be hard, and making money easily always sounded like it's too good to be true... Quick, easy money just sounds like you need to scam others to get it.

But what's wrong with making money easily, if it's done ethically and legally? Wouldn't it be a great thing if money could come to you as easily as possible?

The day you decide to shift your beliefs and understand that it can be easy to generate wealth, your world will start to change for the better.

Roger Bannister, a British athlete, broke the world record on 6th May 1954 by doing what most thought was impossible – he became the first person to run a mile in just four minutes. Before he achieved it, countless athletes attempted to achieve it, and it was concluded that nobody would ever be able to break the four minute barrier after spending decades trying.

But once he did it, people started to believe that it was possible for them too. And just 46 days later after Roger Bannister's feat, John Landy, an Australian runner, not only achieved it but even surpassed the result at 3 minutes 58 seconds. A year later, three runners broke the four minutes barrier in a single race. As of today, more than 1,600 athletes succeeded in breaking the four-minute mile barrier.

That's exactly how most humans are – they refuse to believe certain results are possible, until they start to see people achieving it. That's when the shift in belief happens, before they begin to take action.

And here's the good news for you – way before you, millions of people have already achieved success in changing their lives through real estate investments! It is indeed possible to generate 6-figures and even 7-figures of wealth to help you achieve a carefree lifestyle without worries.

So start believing today, and the next step will help you to get there...

3. **ACTION – I WILL DO WHAT IS NEEDED TO GET WHAT I WANT!**

The final step is to take action, which is the last hurdle for you to cross.

With a strong desire and belief, what you need next is to gain more clarity with your investment options. Start planning for what you want to achieve, lay out your goals, and begin to study the property market.

Roger Bannister desired to achieve the four-minute mile, believed that he would be the first one to do it, and then **he trained hard for it.** Months and months of training, physical conditioning, and practice resulted in one of the greatest feats ever achieved in mankind's history.

Nothing happens without taking action – you don't become a better basketball player just by watching Michael Jordan on YouTube and not practicing on the court.

Similarly, you aren't going to become a successful investor if you just read this book, watch tonnes of investment-related videos, but ultimately not take action in the end.

There is a golden saying: "Buy real estate and wait, don't wait to buy real estate".

Some may say this is just what realtors use to convince people to buy, but this statement will never fail. Property prices in Singapore generally appreciate over time, and those who didn't buy earlier often tend to lament years later that they should have gone ahead with the purchase instead of missing out on the healthy profits.

Astute investors know that time is money, and they don't waste any time. They do their research and homework, speak to experienced realtors for advice, and then take massive action to maximise their returns. They know that there will always be little noises in their head attempting to discourage them, but it doesn't stop them from going ahead to invest in what they believe in.

However, the biggest obstacle you will face in taking action is not just the little noises you hear in your head… I'll talk more about that in the next few secrets that I'm about to share with you.

Go on, flip the page.

Secret #2 – Top 5 Poor Habits That Hold You Back From Riches

In the previous secret, you learnt that success first begins with your mind – and in 3 simple steps: Desire, Belief and Action, you are already setting yourself out to be on the right path for your own success.

However, the journey ahead is still filled with plenty of challenges and obstacles; the 3 steps that you just learnt aren't enough to help you avoid pitfalls and potential mistakes.

To navigate through the path ahead, one of the greatest obstacles comes from poor habits that you may have – some of which you may not even be aware of.

These poor habits are like thieves in the night; they creep in silently into your life, and steal away your rightful wealth. Even when you've made more money, you just can't seem to be able to keep the wealth – your money will end up flowing out somewhere else instead of piling up and growing. Sounds familiar?

Perhaps, you've experienced this before (or are even experiencing it now)…

If you want to avoid losing your wealth to the secret "thieves in the night", you need to identify these poor habits and negative beliefs, and eradicate them out of your life NOW.

(You may not have all of these habits, but if any of it resonates with you, then consider this an opportunity to start turning your life around.)

1. **Negative Association With Money.**

    One of the most detrimental habits that a person could have, is to look at money as if it is not meant to be yours. Worse still, some feel that it is even wrong to be rich!

    "Money is the root of all evil…"

"Filthy, dirty money…"

"Don't be like those stinking rich!"

Even in movies and TV shows, they tend to portray the rich as being the ultimate evil that commoners have to fight against.

I don't disagree that in this world, there are indeed wealthy people who are greedy, manipulative and probably even unethical.

However, there are also many rich and wealthy who are generous, kind-hearted and sincere in person, and they are nothing close to being evil or unscrupulous. Some of them may even be the nicest people you'll ever meet!

In order for you to live a life of abundance and riches, you need to embrace the idea of being rich.

You must believe that being rich is a GOOD thing – because it improves not just your own life, but also the lives of others around you.

Having more money means that you can provide a more comfortable lifestyle for your loved ones. It also means less stress over finances, which contributes to an overall better health and personal well-being.

Once you learn and accept that it is perfectly okay for you to be rich, your world will no longer be the same – money is now your new best friend!

Later in Secret #4 of this book, I will dive deeper into the topic of Wealth Attraction and you will learn more about how you can attract the wealth that you want.

But first, you must really want it, and not harbour any negative association with money.

2. Spending Future Money

Now, this one is serious.

When I talk about spending future money, I'm referring to those who commit to an investment out of misplaced confidence about their incoming finances.

This could potentially be very dangerous, especially if there is no concrete certainty that your future money is confirmed to arrive on time as it should. Just because a huge sum of money is due to come in the future doesn't mean you need to start thinking about spending them now.

There was a buyer who decided to purchase an investment property, and went ahead to purchase thinking that his future funds were secured and guaranteed to come in time for the payments due to the developer. The entire payment timeline and financial calculations were done meticulously to ensure that nothing would go amiss – the whole plan seemed so secure and risk-free. What could possibly go wrong?

Well, months later, Covid-19 happened.

The pandemic resulted in a worldwide economic setback, and the incoming funds were no longer able to come in on time. Worse still, the buyer's income was also affected, resulting in an inevitable withdrawal from the property purchase. Thankfully, the cancellation penalty involved was only around $20,000 – a reasonable amount that was still affordable for him.

While Covid was an unexpected occurrence, it taught us a huge lesson – spending your "future money" always comes with risks.

In 2022, many people got their hands burnt due to the unexpected cryptocurrency meltdown caused by the Terra Luna crash. Billions worldwide lost their investment overnight – some even invested their life savings in it and committed suicide when they realised their savings were completely lost in such a short time.

The crypto meltdown also resulted in many property investors withdrawing from their property purchases, as their expected future funds from cryptocurrency investments went down the drain. Some incurred 6 figures of losses from pulling out of the property purchase – and this is a painful lesson that I hope you can learn from.

If you are one of those who tend to take risks with investments using your future money too, then I would advice you to stop doing so.

Invest within your means, using funds that are already there for your use.

3. **Spending More On Liabilities**

"Rule One. You must know the difference between an asset and a liability, and buy assets. An asset is something that puts money in my pocket. A liability is something that takes money out of my pocket." – Robert Kiyosaki

There are some people who don't understand the concepts of assets and liabilities. They simply just spend and buy things based on their emotions – I like it, I can afford it, and therefore I buy it.

Smart investors know that it is never wise to do so, and so shouldn't you.

Before you buy that luxury car, expensive watch, or spend extravagantly on an expensive meal in a restaurant, you need to think twice. Does any of these help to put more money in your pocket?

Now, I'm not saying that you totally shouldn't enjoy life the way you want to.

I indulge myself too in luxury shopping and expensive food; but most of my money is spent on investments and assets. While spending on liabilities, I spend comfortably knowing that my assets are working for me, and generating more money than I spend.

If you are spending what you earn more on liabilities than assets, then something is not right.

4. **Over-focused On Saving Money**

From a young age, most of us are taught that saving money is important.

Probably one of the early gifts you received as a child was a piggy bank (or something equivalent) – it was our parents' way of teaching us to develop a habit of saving.

There is nothing wrong with saving money. On the contrary, it is indeed a virtue that should be rightly lauded – there are too many people who don't even save a penny of what they earn, and these people tend to suffer most when their finances go south.

However, saving money is not everything.

The amount you can save is dependent on how much wealth you can generate – the more you earn, the more you get to save.

Yet the majority of the world's population focus more on scrimping and saving, instead of thinking how they can generate more wealth!

The key to achieving any form of result is concentrated focus – Tiger Woods became one of the world's greatest golfers because of his concentrated focus while training and practising his swings. David Beckham was known as one of the best free-kick takers in football because of his concentrated focus in practising his free-kicks.

What you focus on for a prolonged, consistent period of time will eventually yield you the desired outcome.

Hence in similar manners, concentrated focus on generating wealth will simply help you to generate more wealth!

This is a very easy concept to understand, but difficult for most to execute – mainly because of a reluctance to face their fear of being poor. That's why they spend more time thinking about how to scrimp and save – which grows their savings but not their wealth.

Here's a simple example to illustrate the difference between savings & wealth generation:

Let's say you earn $5,000 a month, and decide to save $1,500 monthly in your bank account. Each year you save $18,000 and in 10 years that becomes $180,000. Sounds good?

Now let's put the same $1,500 a month to invest in something that generates you 5% compounded interest per annum. In the same period of 10 years, the total wealth accumulated would be $226,402.07 – that's at least $46,000 more than what you would have gotten by purely saving it in your bank account!

This is exactly why investors invest. They focus on wealth generating activities that make the same money work harder for them, and now they have even more money to save.

5. **Complaining About Big Spenders**

Possibly the most common poor habit and least picked up on – often we would hear the poor say things like these:

"What a waste of money!"...

"Why would someone pay so much for this?"...

"I'm not going to pay this kind of crazy price!"...

If these are what you tend to say, stop doing that now!

Big spenders spend big for a reason.

Some may say it's for vanity, to show off, to flaunt their wealth. How do you justify why some products are sold so much more expensive than their cheaper counterparts?

After all, why is there a need to spend $30,000 on a Rolex when you can buy a watch that tells the same time for less than $10?

Why do people drive luxury cars that cost easily at least 3 to 5 times the price of a typical Japan-made sedan?

Here are some reasons why:

When you spend big on luxury, you are paying for quality, for a superior experience.

Just imagine that you just ended work after a long, hectic day. The stress started to get to you, and you couldn't wait to get home… and the car you drive home is a luxurious Mercedes E-Class. Imagine the comfortable leather seats, the spacious cabin, and the smooth enjoyable drive that helped to take some stress away from you… The last thing you want after a stressful day at work is to go home on a bumpy, uncomfortable ride that probably even stinks.

That's what people pay for. A luxury car is no longer just a means of transport – it is also a stress-reliever, a solution to some people's pains.

The rich are also willing to spend more if it helps to save them something much more valuable than money itself – which is TIME.

I personally experienced this myself when I went to Universal Studios Singapore, and opted for their VIP Experience. The VIP Experience costs about 3 times more than the usual adult admission tickets, but it entitled me to skip every single queue for all the rides – I got to even be ahead of those in the Express Queue!

It was amusing (and also alarming) for me to observe how thousands of people don't value their time… they were willing to queue for up to even 2 hours for a ride, while all it took for me was a mere 2 minutes to get into the ride ahead of everyone else.

For some of the rides, we even repeated it more than once back to back – and some of those in the queue looked back at us in disgust when they realised we were about to take the ride a second time...

This experience taught me one thing. The poor love complaining about the rich, but they don't get that time is more valuable than money. I went for the VIP Experience not to flaunt or show off – I simply wanted to spend less time queueing. Instead of arriving at the theme park at 10am like most others, we arrived at 1.30pm (which meant more sleeping time in the morning) – and we left before 6pm after completing all the rides we wanted to try while the rest of the visitors continued to play in the theme park till it closed at 7.

Between saving money and saving time, the rich will always tend to choose time. Because money lost can always be earned back, but time lost will always be lost.

The above examples are just a few of the many valid reasons why the rich spend more; when you learn to value things the way richer people do, you will become one of them.

But if you complain about those who spend big, you are telling the Universe that you don't want to be rich.

So think twice before you complain again.

In the 5 poor habits that I shared with you above, if any of it does resonate with you, then I am truly happy for you – this is the first step towards changing your life with the increased awareness you now have.

Why are these important for any real estate investor?

I'm sharing all these with you so that you can be successful not just in your investments, but to also turn yourself into a true wealth magnet.

After all, making money is one thing; it is another skill to retain your wealth and attract even more to you!

What I have shared so far in the first 2 secrets are nothing complex or difficult, and I won't blame you if you think that it's too simple to be effective for you. However, if you do spend some time observing people around you, then you will begin to see that the exact negative traits and poor habits I shared are actually very commonplace. The poorer these people are, the more of these traits you will find in them.

What is seen cannot be unseen – you are now aware of these bad habits that you should avoid at all cost, and now the responsibility is on you to make sure you do not fall back into the same habits again.

In the next secret, what you will learn is even more crucial to the success of your real estate investments…

Secret #3 – The Friendly Housing Advice You Should Never Take

Most real estate investors I've met do not act alone.

They would turn to their loved ones, close friends and colleagues, seeking advice and opinions.

While there is absolutely nothing wrong with seeking for alternative opinion and advice, it can also be dangerous to do so if you do not get the advice that is truly helpful for you.

My rationale here is straightforward: your real estate investment would usually cost you at least 6 figures in downpayment, with a property price of likely more than $1 million dollars involved. Why take the risk listening to non-professionals?

Your family, friends and colleagues may care a lot about you, and that's a great thing to have. But if anything goes wrong with the investment, you would not be able to hold any of them responsible, would you?

Some of them may be advising you based on their past experiences – these can be good references for you, but I would also advice you to exercise caution. What used to work (or not work) for them may not be applicable for your own investments because every property buyers' needs and requirements differ, and the property market last time may not work the same way as the property market today.

Here are some common housing advice from people around you that I would advice you to never take:

1. **Just buy HDB flat, why must you buy a condo?**

    This would be a very common advice usually from the elderly, and that's understandable. After all, during their time, most of them benefited from the healthy profits gained from selling their HDB flats.

Those were the days when a HDB flat was bound to appreciate in price, and it was a tried-and-tested route for many of the older generation.

However, their advice comes mainly from a place of fear – they are mostly afraid that condo investments would bring higher risks due to the higher outlay, and they would not want to see you suffer. Perhaps, they had seen the days when the property market crashed big time, such as during the 1997 Asian Financial Crisis, or in 2008 due to the Lehman Brothers Crisis.

Much as they are advising you with good intentions, my personal opinion is that HDB flats are not meant for investment purposes.

While it is true that HDB flats may still appreciate in price, one golden principle will never change: HDB Flats are meant to remain affordable, as they are still public housing and remain heavily regulated by the government.

If you're looking to buy just to have a roof over your head, with more space and comfort for a lower price, then yes a HDB flat would make sense for you.

But if what you want is to have a higher certainty of capital appreciation, with a shorter tie-down period before you should sell, then a private property would be a clearer choice. Don't worry about the potential risks, I will cover more about that later in this book.

In Secret #15, I will also share the ugly truths about public housing that you may not know, and it would be even clearer for you why going for a HDB flat isn't as safe as what some people assumed it to be.

2. **Buy Freehold, Confirm Won't Go Wrong!**

Ahhhh, the old cliché.

Firstly, I would like to say that I'm not against freehold. In fact, I'm staying in a freehold property myself, and I can relate to those who are die-hard believers of freehold estates.

Freehold properties are highly sought-after, simply because its lease would never expire, hence giving the illusion that the resale price wouldn't drop much and the profits would be virtually guaranteed.

Unfortunately, there are freehold property owners who suffered even millions in losses (such as Scotts Square), and there are also many freehold developments that failed to achieve breakeven price in the resale market even after more than 10 years.

This is the truth: there are freehold properties that are excellent investments, and there are those that failed miserably. Similarly, there are leasehold properties that out-perform freehold properties of the same age, and there are also leasehold properties that failed to generate profits too.

You see, it's not always about whether it's freehold or not.

Freehold status is not an immunity shield that protects you from depreciation – it's merely one of the factors that help to attract prospective buyers. But a property's potential profits is not entirely reliant on whether it's freehold – there are so many more factors that buyers have to consider about, which is why you shouldn't just blindly focus solely on freehold properties for your investment.

My advice is to keep an open mind, and never rule out leasehold properties. Look at developments objectively, and weigh out the various pros and cons through a fair comparison, then decide on what is best for you.

In Secret #18, I will cover in detail the reasons why some Freehold properties fail, and in Secret #24 you will learn the strategies you can use to invest in the most suitable property, be it Freehold or Leasehold.

Until then, hold your judgments.

3. **Buy resale condo, it's cheaper and safer!**

   Again, another subjective advice.

   Cheaper doesn't always mean it is safer, and identifying a good investment property is more than just the pricing.

   Personally, I am not against buying resale properties. I've brought my own clients to purchase resale properties before, even for pure investment purposes.

   Even so, I would not go to the extent to claim that resale properties are always the best options, because once again there are many factors to consider other than just looking at the price alone. Likewise, I wouldn't say that you should go for a new launch condo right away.

   End of the day it depends on your investment objectives and the financial considerations – for some people, a new launch condo would work best, and for some a resale property would be more ideal.

   Some may advice you to go for a resale property because they had relatives or friends staying there sitting on healthy paper-gains, or probably already sold off for their handsome profits.

   But what they did not factor in was the entry price that those owners entered at, versus the entry price you would be entering into.

   Did they study the resale transaction volume? The recent price trends? What's popular in the development and what's not? Which layout is more preferred by buyers? Is the development doing better than their neighbours nearby?

   If they can't give you a clear and concise analysis, then their advice is nothing more than just a personal opinion, and I wouldn't bet a million-dollar property investment based on a personal opinion.

   In Secret #17, I will share why buying cheaper properties may not make you wealthier – the factual data could possibly blow your mind.

The above 3 examples are the most common advice given by people around you – there may be more advice that they would give, but I believe by now you would understand the most important point: don't take the advice of non-professionals.

Again, I understand their kind intentions. They care about you and have your best interests at heart. However, if you want to be a successful investor, you need to work with industry experts who have the knowledge and experience to advice you in the most objective manner possible.

Cristiano Ronaldo might not have been the football player he is today without the guidance of Sir Alex Ferguson. Michael Jordan would not have achieved true greatness without the coaching from Phil Jackson. Even Bill Gates was mentored by Warren Buffett – no matter how much of a genius you are, there will always be knowledge that you can learn from a coach or mentor who is an expert in a field that you are yet to be.

If you have such a person in your personal circle, that would be awesome – not everyone is blessed with opportunities to learn from expert investors in close proximity.

But otherwise, go seek professional advice.

Now turn over to the next page for more life-changing secrets that will attract even more wealth to you.

Secret #4 – The Little-Known Truths About Wealth Attraction

Wealth.

A simple yet complex word.

Many people chase after it, yet so little can obtain it. Why is that so?

Let's think about this for a moment – wealth is definitely one of the most important topics that should have been taught in schools, yet it is not so.

In any formal education system you can find in the world, they do not teach any subjects related to wealth. Not even in business school!

The real truth is this: the formal education system was designed to keep people poor.

Yes, you heard me right.

The schools don't teach you anything about wealth, because the purpose of schools was not to produce more entrepreneurs; the main objective was to produce more manpower for businesses to employ.

From 1760 to 1840, the Industrial Revolution in Great Britain, the United States of America and Europe meant that more workers were needed to support the industrial workforce.

Hence, more schools were set up with the aim of grooming batches of ready workers to work in factories. Strict rules were enforced not just to maintain discipline, but to also train people to follow strict instructions so that they become obedient followers.

Fast forward to the education system in Singapore today - only in top elite schools would the students be exposed to ideas of entrepreneurship and be encouraged to start their own businesses.

Even so, there is still no emphasis on the topic of wealth.

So most people continue to believe that the best pathway in life is to study their way up, get a university degree, and then climb up the corporate ladder step by step, working their ass off just to pay off their study loans first… Not to mention planning for housing, marriage next…

Think about this cycle.

You deposit your savings in the bank. The bank lends the money to the wealthy, who then uses that money to start up a business, and then you get hired by that same business. All the time and money you spent was just meant to help the wealthy become wealthier.

The only true winner? The wealthy.

And there's absolutely nothing wrong with this cycle – such is the true nature of life.

97% of the world's population are working their socks off just to feed the wealthy top 3%, and that will always remain the case.

If you're one of those who took the typical route that I mentioned above, do understand that I do not mean to dampen your mood or dash your "dreams" on purpose. I'm just speaking the truth for what it is, so that you can wake up from "reality" to see the real reality.

My parents were one of those who took the typical route, and they desperately wanted to make sure that I end up with a university degree. They kept saying that having a degree is always a good back-up plan in life that will keep me employed with a better salary than most, especially in today's competitive society. Not having a degree was seen as a huge disadvantage to them.

Well, I did attend university… but I did not complete it.

I simply stopped going to school. Not because I didn't like studying, nor was it because I was struggling. On the contrary, my grades were pretty good.

The main reason why I stopped my university studies was a straightforward one – I just don't fancy working for someone else, making another rich man richer while I remain stuck on a fixed payroll with no certainty of job security.

No matter what people say, having a degree isn't a real back-up plan. In times of economic crisis and recession, no one's job could be truly secure.

The Covid-19 pandemic proved just that – many big brands such as Forever 21, Victoria's Secret went bust. Restaurants and entertainment clubs were put out of business due to prolonged lockdowns, and the travel industry took a huge hit when the world simply stopped travelling for almost 2 full years.

Where's the security and certainty in times like these?

True wealth isn't defined by your educational qualifications nor your occupation; it is how you view time and money that determines the wealth you attract in your life.

As you've learnt in Secret #2, the rich value Time the most.

If you observe carefully, you will see that rich people buy time, and poor people sell time.

That's why big bosses pay salaries to hire people to work for them, so that they can generate higher revenue without having to sacrifice too much time working. Meanwhile, the poor are the ones who sell their time for money, and they remain trapped in this scenario because of their fear of losing their jobs.

If you are one of those who are stuck in a job today, it is still not too late to decide to change your life.

You can only attract true wealth when you start to value your time; this is why top business consultants charge at least 5 figures per hour to guide business owners to be on the right track, and also why top personal coaches like Tony Robbins can charge more than USD$1 million to do 1 on 1 coaching.

So how much do you think your time is worth? Are you really paid well enough to justify the time you spent at work?

Now, I'm not asking you to quit your job immediately to be an entrepreneur right away. That would be financially irresponsible to do so, and it would put you and your family into a highly stressful situation unnecessarily.

However, you should start thinking about investing in assets such as real estate to generate your first pot of gold, and then leverage on healthy returns from the investments to grow your wealth.

The first goal is to achieve financial independence (which means you no longer rely on your salary to make a living), and set aside savings to start your own business someday to scale your income.

Even if being an entrepreneur does not interest you, in the very least you would have achieved greater financial control. If you can follow the advice laid out in this book, I'm certain that you will be on your way to be financially free eventually.

In Secret #29, you will even learn the Million-Dollar Retirement Blueprint, with a step-by-step framework that teaches you how you can leverage on property investments to retire with more than $1 million in your bank account.

But before that, go on to the next chapter and understand why Singapore's Real Estate holds the key to your investment success.

CHAPTER 2

SINGAPORE, THE REAL ESTATE GOLD MINE

This island state was destined to make you rich, only if you could see it...

Secret #5 – Limited Land, Unlimited Wealth

Singapore is a country that you can hardly see on the world map.

The approximate size of the entire country is only around 728 square kilometres, which is only around 90% of the size of the entire New York City!

Despite being a small island state, Singapore ranks among the top cities in the world with first-world infrastructure and an extremely high home-ownership rate of 88.9% as of the end of 2021.

This is exactly why real estate in Singapore is so highly sought-after; with such limited land supply, land becomes a precious and rare commodity. This becomes a huge advantage for investors, as rising land costs would become inevitable, thereby contributing to a constant growth in real estate prices.

However, having limited land is just part of the equation – it is also the political stability and stable economy that puts Singapore as among the wealthiest countries in the world, hence attracting many multinational companies to expand their business here. Major corporations such as Google, Facebook, Rolls Royce and Dyson, just to name a few, have established their Asian-Pacific headquarters in tiny little Singapore.

Being a small nation, Singapore overcame many challenges – there were no natural resources, with a limited supply of land and water, and the country is so small that a single nuclear bomb could possibly wipe out the entire country. It was truly no mean feat for Singapore to be where they are today – a highly respected nation that successfully balanced diplomatic ties with both China and America, and evolved into a first-world country in less than 50 years of independence.

As an investor, if you understand the concept of supply and demand, then Singapore's real estate market should easily appeal to you.

Since Singapore has a limited supply, all we need is to have demand outweighing supply to help encourage real estate price growth. So where would the demand come from?

With an existing population of 5.4 million people (as of 2022), the government is actually still looking to grow their population further. Back in 2013, the government announced the Population White Paper (PWP), in which they laid out the vision of achieving up to 6.9 million in population by year 2030.

Why do we need so many people in Singapore?

The answer is simple – the Singapore government is fighting against the issues of an ageing population.

Look at the diagram above – this is Singapore's current population demographics as of the end of 2021. It is now shaped like a diamond, with the majority of the population currently in their mid 30s to 50s.

At the rate of how it's going, by 2030 we could possibly see the diagram turning into an inverted triangle instead.

When that happens, it would mean that we have too many elderly citizens, and too few working adults to support the elderly.

That would directly affect Singapore's Gross Domestic Product (GDP) growth, which is exactly why the government is so concerned about the ageing population issue!

So let's assume that we do achieve 6.9 million population by 2030. Considering that Singapore's birth rates and death rates are quite close (crude birth rate stands at 8.6 per 1000 population, crude death rates stand at 5.8 per 1000 population), we are not able to rely purely on natural births to increase the population by so many in such a short time.

The solution? Foreign imports.

To be more exact, WEALTHY foreign imports.

That's why in January 2020, Singapore's government rolled out the Global Investor Programme (GIP) to attract Ultra High Net-Worth individuals and families, offering them fast-track access to apply for Permanent Residency (PR) status in Singapore.

Now let's do some simple math.

Given that the average household size in Singapore stands at approximately 3.15 persons per household, for 1.5 million new citizens we would require at least 476,190 homes to be built by 2030.

That makes it more than 59,000 new homes to be built every year from now on… and the current average number of new homes built per year stands at between 10,000 to 25,000 homes on average.

Unless the government drastically increases land supply for developers to purchase, at this moment there is a huge shortage of supply for the incoming population… Do you see where I'm going with this?

Yes, it's back to the theory of supply versus demand.

The magic formula behind Singapore's real estate success is simply this:

Limited Land Supply + High Demand From Incoming Population Growth = Higher Real Estate Prices.

Added with the political and economic stability that I mentioned earlier, this becomes a recipe that you can rely on to generate more wealth!

Of course, that doesn't mean that every property in Singapore is profitable. But at least on a macro level, you can be assured that Singapore is one of the best countries that you can invest in.

Furthermore, the government tends to look after the rich and wealthy here… I'll talk more about that in the next Secret.

Secret #6 – Why The Rich Loves The Government

Before I begin, the content below bears no allegiance to any particular political party – it is my personal opinion purely formed from my observations and understanding. You can choose to disagree with my opinion, that's okay. Just know that whatever I share here is meant to share with you a different perspective.

Very often, we would hear the poor complain about the government. This is unfortunately a universal fact – in any part of the world, the poor are often the ones who make the most noises about the government.

I'm not an expert with politics, but I can be certain that it's never easy to govern poor people.

No matter how much support the government provided, how much fundings and grants was disbursed, and how many policies they came up with to help people, there would still be discontentment and displeasure.

That's because there are always people who lack gratitude, and are never truly content with what they get. These people continue to demand for more, as if they had contributed a lot to the nation.

Now, it isn't that I have no empathy for the poor. It is just that I recognise the difficulties that the government faces, and at the same time I've observed the complaints poor people make – it's always about how life has been unfair to them, how the government wasn't taking good care of them, and then they accept that this is going to be their life – albeit in a disgruntled manner.

Yet, they don't take the right action to get themselves out of poverty.

Some think that by working hard and saving more, they would get out of poverty... but you and I both know that this is never going to be enough. Inflation alone will render the hard-earned savings irrelevant in a matter of years; that's why we need to invest our money wisely.

Imagine that you are the owner of a business.

In your company, there are staff who are highly-motivated, and generate a lot of income for you through sales. On the other hand, there are also staff who are less productive, don't make much money for you, and complain all the time.

Who would you spend more time, resources and money on?

It is a no-brainer that in the corporate world, the better performers get more opportunities and are duly rewarded for their contributions to the company, while the poor performers simply just get fired eventually.

Thankfully, in Singapore the government still takes good care of the poor. Majority of the population at least have a roof over their head, with access to medical support, financial support, and could easily reach out to a wide variety of welfare groups that were set up to assist the poor and needy.

During 2020 to 2022, Singapore's government spent over SGD $6 Billion on Covid-related fundings – yet the poor continue to complain.

Some might argue and say that a government should take care of all citizens, regardless of whether they are rich or poor...

While that is theoretically not wrong, the poor's reliance on the government for their own survival will only keep them stuck in poverty.

Think about a lion that was raised in a zoo; for its whole life, the lion was fed by zookeepers. It never had to hunt for food, and over many years of domestication, the lion became reliant on the regular feedings. If you put this lion back into the wild, it will not survive for long because the hunting ability is blunted; if given a choice this lion would rather be back in the zoo and be caged for life, if it meant that there's always food to ensure its survival.

That lion represents poor people, the zookeeper represents the government.

I'm sure you get what I mean now.

Now think of Singapore's government as a smart, astute businessman.

All this businessman wants is to make the country more wealthy and prosperous... and a smart businessman will know that retaining the top performers who contribute the most to the company's revenue is key to everlasting success.

So what does the government do to retain the rich and wealthy citizens?

They help them to become even wealthier.

It's a known fact that in Singapore, business taxes are considered one of the lowest among well-established nations. Corporate headline tax rate in Singapore was reduced to just 17% since 2010 till now; in comparison, corporate tax in Japan, Australia and Germany stands at 30% today, in China and South Korea it's 25%, in neighbouring country Malaysia it's 24%, and even in United States of America the corporate tax rate is at 21%.

This is yet to also include tax exemptions for new start-up companies in Singapore, such as the 75% exemption for the first $100,000 earned, and a 50% exception for the next $100,000.

Also, the government seeks to help businesses grow by creating more job opportunities. Being a country with no natural resources, not even water, the only way to survive is to create more job opportunities to retain talents and also attract foreign talents at the same time.

When Marina Bay Sands (MBS) and Resorts World Sentosa (RWS) were completed in 2010, both Integrated Resorts (IR) created more than 20,000 direct employment, out of which over 65% employed were locals.

Unknown to many, there is also an existing plan for Greater One-North, to expand the existing industries in the One-North estate to provide 120,000 jobs, which would account for 5% of Singapore's overall employment.

These few examples illustrate how the government literally creates wealth for businesses – by providing more job opportunities, businesses can expand and employ more manpower to scale their business growth, therefore helping business owners to generate higher revenue.

In turn, the rich contribute back to the country (some willingly and some not) with tax money – the highest income tax rate being 24%, and the highest property tax for a non-owner occupied property is 36% of the annual value (the lowest being a mere 12%).

No matter how much people like to complain, let's not forget that the fundings and support given to the poor from the government comes from taxpayers' money, and the biggest contributors to taxes are the rich & wealthy that most poor people scorn upon.

Find some time today and go out for a walk.

Observe the beautiful trees lined up along the roads that make every drivers' day a more pleasant one...

Look at the meticulously planned transport system, with increased connectivity being improved all the time.

Walk along the streets and see how clean our pavements are, with regular cleaning done.

Not to forget the safe and secure environment that we live in, with low crime rates that allows you to go home peacefully every day...

Most Singaporeans take these for granted – and these factors are key contributions to maintaining the attractiveness of Singapore's real estate market, with good governance and constant improvements to housing estates.

I once hosted an American friend named Terry, who spent half his life living in New York and the other half in Tokyo. He made a comment that I would never forget:

"Singapore is so well-planned, it's like Disneyland! But y'all know that in Disneyland, nothing comes cheap..."

That was so spot on.

Singapore is indeed an expensive place to live in, but if given a choice I would still prefer to stay in this beautiful "Disneyland" of a country... A country where the government looks after both the poor and the rich, and uses the rich's money to improve infrastructure so that businesses can thrive and real estate can prosper.

However, there are still certain aspects that I disagree with... Turn to the next Secret now and you'll soon understand why.

Secret #7 – What You Read Is Not Always Real

On 16th December 2021, the government rolled out a series of cooling measures as means to cool down the property market price.

Total Debt Servicing Ratio (TDSR) was adjusted from 60% to 55%, and Additional Buyer's Stamp Duties (ABSD) were increased across the board for locals and Permanent Residents (PR) seeking to invest in their 2nd and 3rd properties, as well as for higher stamp duties for foreigners (increased from 20% to 30%).

Back then, the widespread perception was that property prices were going to start falling.

One day, I was contacted by a news reporter working for a reputable news channel.

The reporter wanted to interview me about the cooling measures, but prior to the formal interview she asked me briefly for my take on the impact of the new measures.

I told her that the cooling measures would have very minimal impact on the property prices, as the measures would only affect a small minority of the population. My prediction was that property prices would continue to climb upwards, albeit at a slower pace.

After hearing my opinion, the reporter never got back to me again about the formal interview.

Subsequently, the media continued to spread the perception of the property market cooling down, urging buyers to exercise caution if they intend to invest in any property.

In the end, transaction volume did fall as many buyers remained sceptical about the property market, but property prices did not drop. Just as I predicted, the prices held up and continued to climb upwards slowly, even when there were much less transactions.

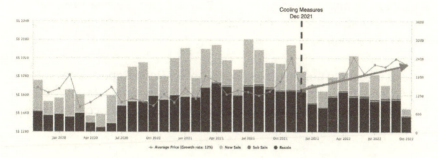

Source: EdgeProp, URA

This is exactly why I always tell my clients not to blindly follow what the media says – what they read from the news may not always be real.

More often than not, the media prefers to focus more on the negatives, and it is not just for real estate. Flip through the pages of a newspaper, and you will find more negative news than positive ones.

Why is that so?

The reason is simple – negative news sells.

Unfortunately, people who are hooked on reading newspapers also tend to be more fearful, as their subconscious mind becomes increasingly exposed to negative news that constantly plants the seeds of fear and uncertainty.

In Solomon Islands, the native tribes do not simply just cut down a tree. They would surround the tree and curse at it for hours every day… and within weeks, the tree simply dries up and becomes dead. This is how negativity works; if even a tree can die from constant exposure to negative energy, what about a human mind that's constantly exposed to negative news?

I'm not saying that you should completely avoid the news, but it would be wise to be selective with the news you read. It's always good to keep up with current affairs and matters of the world, but do avoid negative news whenever possible.

For instance, instead of reading The Straits Times, I prefer to follow The Business Times – there's simply less negativity and less sensationalism in their news reporting.

Instead of reading gossip magazines, I opt for Robb Report instead. Robb Report is a magazine that is focused on luxury products and affluent lifestyles for the rich and wealthy, which expands your subconscious mind even more to attract the wealth you want.

As an investor, you need to guard your mind and your heart, and not be swayed by what most people's knee-jerk reactions to what the media says.

Warren Buffett once said: "Be fearful when others are greedy, and be greedy when others are fearful".

This line couldn't be more apt when it is applied to real estate investments.

In times when most are fearful about buying real estate, that's the best time for you to buy. When most are frantically buying, that's when you should not enter.

I know this may sound counter-intuitive, but it is true.

When the media tells you not to buy, you buy. Because when transaction volume drops, housing developers and home sellers will be less bullish about their selling price. On the contrary, when the market is hot, the developers and sellers hold the upper hand with their pricing!

That's why smart investors know that it is important not to believe everything you hear or read from the media. Instead, you should do your own research to determine what's good to invest in and not.

You might be thinking that doing your own research is easier said than done. Where can you obtain the right information and data that you need?

What if I tell you that the most important information you need is actually hidden in plain sight? It has never been easier to obtain these key information for FREE…

You'll get the answer in the next Secret.

Secret #8 – The Path To Gold Is Hidden In Plain Sight

Real estate investment today is very much different from what it used to be in the past.

Thanks to the creation of the internet, and subsequently the birth of search engines such as Google, property buyers today have easy access to more information than ever.

Investors today are much more savvy than investors from a decade ago, simply because in the past there was less data available (and also less accessible to the common public).

In the past, investors relied heavily on realtors for advice and insights. Unfortunately, most realtors back then were also less-educated, and a lot of their sales come from emotional selling rather than relying on facts and figures.

Today, with an increased emphasis on data and research, real estate agencies also began to conduct more consumer seminars to share their insights based on analytical data. Top realtors will be able to share with you data-driven insights, while you can also easily subscribe for property data to get quick access to the information you need.

However, not every information requires a paid subscription for access.

What I'm about to share with you is actually available for FREE, and most realtors rely on these free tools to make a living. These tools would help you to spot high potential estates that you can invest in, and also have a clear overview of the behaviour trends and demographics of real estate buyers, which would help you greatly in making a more informed decision for your own investments.

Interestingly, many of these tools have been around for a long time… and yet their existence remains unknown to many. You may have come across a few of them before, but there might just be a few that are new to you too.

1. **URA Master Plan**
   https://www.ura.gov.sg/maps/

   The Master Plan is one of the most essential tools for realtors and property investors. Introduced by the Urban Redevelopment Authority (URA), the Master Plan reveals the key planning decisions for every single estate in Singapore. This provides a huge insight into the government's vision for the country, and you will be able to know in advance the future transformations that would be taking place.

   Once every 5 years, the Master Plan will be updated with the latest revisions to maintain its relevance.

   The very first thing you need to learn is to understand the Legend of the plan, and be able to identify the various property types according to its colour codes. This will help you to see what are the potential future developments in every estate, so that you can decide if a property in the estate is worth investing in.

   For instance, if there is a huge empty plot of land beside the property you're interested in, go to the Master Plan and search for that empty land. If the land plot turns out to be purple in colour, it means there would be an industrial building to be built on that land in the future. If the plot is orange, it will be for residential purposes. If the plot is light blue, it will be a mixed development with both commercial and residential components.

   With these useful information, you will be able to spot the future potential of a property very easily.

   Another section that I love playing around with is the Control Plans. It will turn the whole map into black and white – after which you can toggle the filters to study the connectivity plans, where you will be able to see the transport plans and also the outlines of upcoming train stations and train lines.

   If you are keen on buying a landed property, you may also toggle the Landed Housing Area filter under Control Plans to study the various Landed zoning areas. It is specifically indicated in the Master Plan how many storeys you are allowed to build up to, what types of landed properties are in the area, and you can even identify where the Good Class Bungalows clusters are located.

I regard the Master Plan as a "magic crystal ball" – by studying the plan, I can spot where future developments would be, and how it could transform the estate to become more vibrant in years to come. More importantly, I can also identify the potential government land sales that would help to push up the market value of nearby properties. Don't underestimate what insights you can gain from this Master Plan – it could just be the most essential tool that generates wealth for your property investment!

2. **Singapore Department Of Statistics**
   https://www.singstat.gov.sg/

One of the least-known government websites, but possibly the most insightful.

In this powerful website, you will gain access to a huge range of data and information that were compiled and directly published by the government, and it will enlighten you further on the future direction of where the country is heading towards.

Once you get into the website, scroll down and go to the "Visualising Data" section. You will see 6 main themes: Economy, Industry, Trade & Investment, Population, Households, and Society.

I frequently would study the Population and Households themes. You are free to explore any of the 6 themes, but Population and Households would give you the key insights when it comes to real estate investing.

Under Population and Households, there would be many different types of data that you can access. Under each sub-category, you will see that there are interactive dashboards that you can go into. These dashboards are extremely useful in helping you to visualise the data better.

Households and Housing Dashboard

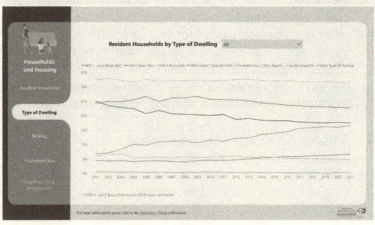

Source: Singapore Department Of Statistics

The above illustration is one of the interactive dashboards under the Households theme. In this chart, you will observe that there is an increasing trend of households moving towards condominiums as shown with the rising green line, and a declining ratio of the households staying in HDB flats. The only rising trend for HDB flats would be the 1-room flats, which is due to the rise of older generation retirees choosing to stay in a small HDB flat to retire in.

This chart alone would already tell you one indisputable truth – there is indeed an increasing demand for condominiums, and this is why most propertyinvestors tend to put their money in private condominiums.

Continue to explore the various data available in the website, and it will open your eyes to many more enlightening truths that you never knew.

3. **URA Media Releases – Quarterly Real Estate Statistics**
   https://www.ura.gov.sg/Corporate/Property/Property-Data

   Yet another essential tool by URA – plenty of useful information lies in their quarterly media releases.

   Scroll down after you enter the website listed above, and you will find the section where URA's media releases are at. Look for the quarterly real estate statistics.

   In the media release, there will be a series of information that you can study, such as the Property Price Index, Rental Index, Total Unsold Supply Of Private Residential In The Pipeline, and more.

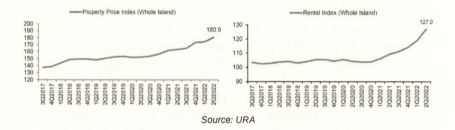

Source: URA

These are extremely useful for you to understand what is going on in the property market today, and to determine if it is a good time to enter the property market or not.

Later in Secret #11, I will also share with you how to time the entry and exit for your property investments in a safe and predictable manner.

But before that, I'd strongly encourage you to spend some time to explore URA's media releases and learn to understand what the data is telling you.

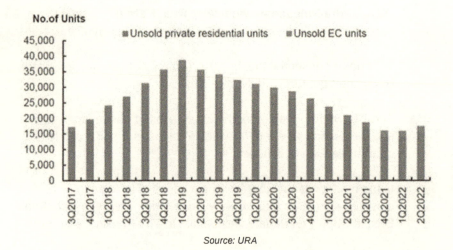

Source: URA

For example, the chart above which is the Total Unsold Supply Of Private Residential In The Pipeline, tells you a very clear picture of a steady decline in available supply in the market.

In Q2 of 2022, there was a slight increase in supply due to the launch of new projects such as AMO Residence, Piccadilly Grand, Liv @ MB just to name a few, but generally the supply available is still significantly less than what it was in 2018 and 2019.

This chart shows why new launch prices didn't come down – with consistent demand and declining supply, most developers would not see the need to reduce their selling price.

That's why smart investors who took action sooner saved both time and money, while those who chose to sit on the fence either entered late at higher prices, or they have yet to even take action at all.

The 3 tools that I shared with you above should adequately allow you to form a clear and concise understanding of Singapore's real estate market movements and direction. These are exactly what I study on a regular basis to help my investor clients gain more clarity for their investments, and it should also help you greatly in similar ways.

The next step for you now is to learn how you can start your investment journey, and I can't wait to share more of that with you in the following chapter!

CHAPTER 3

CLARITY, CERTAINTY, CONFIDENCE

Imagine that you just signed on the dotted line for your property investment... only to start getting cold feet moments later.

There's no way back now, and you begin to lose sleep every single night worrying about the mistake you've just made...

It doesn't have to be this way.

Secret #9 – The 3 Cs Every Investor Needs

Clarity, Certainty, Confidence.

These are the 3 Cs that I stand by, and it became the very core values that helped me to serve my own investor clients. I believe every investor needs these 3 Cs; without any of them, I would not want my client to proceed with any property purchase.

Every property investment involves at least 6-figure, even 7 or 8-figure worth of funds invested… That places a huge responsibility on my shoulders to ensure that the investment plan is a sound one with low risks. Note that I don't promise a risk-free investment, because there's no way anyone can promise it to be zero-risk.

So why these 3 Cs?

Firstly, CLARITY.

This is the first of the 3 Cs, and it is also the most important. Without clarity, how could one possibly think about taking any action? You need to know WHY you are even doing this in the first place!

"A confused mind always says no." says Russell Brunson, founder of ClickFunnels.

This is pretty much a universal law; if there are red flags and warning signals going off in your head, you're not likely to proceed ahead.

So how do we get to more clarity?

To do so, there are a few questions that you need to ask yourself. Self-awareness is the key to your success, because only then will you truly find the motivation and sense of purpose towards your investment plans to generate more wealth.

> **Question 1: Why must you invest your money?**
>
> *Is there a reason why you decided that your money should work harder for you? What triggered you to think about this to begin*

with? If there is an event or incident that occurred to make you think about investing, write it down and elaborate on how it triggered you and why.

Question 2: How much profits (reasonably) should the investment yield in order for it to be considered as a success?

Write down the magic number that you have in mind. Take note that it should be a reasonable, achievable figure, and not an unrealistic sky-high sum.

Question 3: Why do you need this amount of money? What would it be used for?

Is this money for your retirement? For your children's education? Or to set aside for their future housing needs? Be very specific about your purpose. Don't give a generic answer, because money loves it when you have a true purpose for it.

Question 4: What will happen if you don't invest?

Think about the consequences of not investing your money. What will happen a few years down the road? Is your job 100% secure? Can you catch up with the rising cost of inflation? Will your family suffer for it? Write down what you think could be the consequences you have to face.

Question 5: Think about the future you want. What does it look like to you?

What kind of house do you want to stay in? The countries that you want to travel to? The car you want to drive? The places you want to bring your loved ones to? Write down your vision of your dream future, and believe that it will come true.

After you've completed the above 5 questions, you should see more clearly now why it is necessary for you to invest. It is absolutely okay if you don't find your purpose or reasons; maybe it is just not the time yet today.

But if you feel a strong sense of motivation and purpose right now, then I'm truly happy for you! At this stage you've already surpassed most other investors, because the majority of them do not think deep enough about their purpose, and without such clarity some of them will not even take action in the end.

Give yourself a pat on the back, you deserve it!

Now the next C would be CERTAINTY.

This would be a more sophisticated step to take, because certainty is about knowing HOW your investment plans can be executed.

Just imagine as if you're driving overseas in a country that you're visiting for the very first time. You are completely unfamiliar with the roads, and your destination is at least 2 hours' drive away from where you are now. So how do you get there?

Yes, you rely on the help of the GPS in your smartphone. With a few taps, you can get guided directions that will tell you exactly how to get to your destination safely, either in the fastest way or the shortest distance.

The same applies for your real estate investment – you need a realtor to act as your GPS.

If you recall what I shared in Secret #3, you will remember that your loved one and your friends are not the best people to advise you, unless they are realtors or are deeply immersed into the real estate market on a regular basis.

Of course, you might be one of those who are skeptical and do not trust realtors easily, and I do not blame you.

Perhaps, you had a bad experience with a realtor before, or you've met some who didn't do a great job for you.

Perhaps, you have a perception that all realtors want is a big fat commission cheque, and will do everything to make you buy now.

But let's be fair here – there are still realtors out there who put their clients' interest first, and would be able to give you objective advice that is for your own good.

It's just about meeting the right one, and I hope that happens for you.

Do note that it's not about getting one with the most years of experience, because that can be subjective.

A realtor who has been in the industry for more than 10 years may not be guaranteed to be better than a realtor in his first or second year – what if the more "experienced" agent only transacts 2 to 3 small deals a year, compared to a newer agent who works hard and transacts easily 10 or more deals in a year?

Don't judge a realtor by their years in the industry – look at their results achieved, and more importantly if he or she is able to help you achieve the 3 Cs that you need, especially the certainty about your investment.

A good realtor should be able to help you feel more certain about how to execute your investment plans, and here's a guideline on what you should expect your realtor to help you with:

1. **Analyse your finances and affordability thoroughly.**

   Knowing your true affordability does matter. There are buyers who overestimate their affordability, and had to settle for less ideal investment choices than what they hoped for initially. On the flip side, there are also buyers who under-estimate their affordability, resulting in them missing out on better options.

   Some may even be unfamiliar with the latest stamp duties and loan frameworks, so it is important to get the realtor to assess if your finances are healthy enough to proceed with the purchase. They may even be able to help you come up with extra "free money" to purchase the property, which I will cover more details in Secret #12.

2. **Identify all possible routes you can take, including what's next and beyond.**

   Depending on your affordability, the realtor should work out various possibilities for you. It would be best if he or she can identify your full potential, not just for the immediate investment, but also to plan beyond that.

Some examples of the possible routes, depending on individual's needs, would be:

- *Buying 1 property under 2 names for own-stay, and decouple subsequently later to invest in a 2nd property*
- *Buying 2 separate properties right away for couples*
- *Buying a new launch property for capital appreciation*
- *Buying a resale property for immediate rental yield*
- *Buying in Trust using children's names*

And so on...

What I usually do for investors is to map out how they can leverage on their next investment to grow their wealth and possibly even own multiple properties in the future, and map out the exact route to get there. This becomes the roadmap that the investor can follow accordingly.

For example, if your goal is to own a landed property worth at least $8 million in 15 years' time, I will work out the various routes possible to make it a reality, as long as you meet the necessary financial prerequisites to qualify for the methods that I suggest.

For some, they may even be able to generate more than $1 million cash savings and more for their future legacy, to leave behind for the next generation. You can learn more about how you can do so in Secret #29 later in this book.

3. **Share with you the investment angles and methods that are most suitable for you.**

   Once the possibilities are explored, and you've decided on the most feasible route to take, the next step is to identify the best investment angle based on the chosen route.

   Investment angle is more in-depth and specific, right down to the type of property and what kind of location you can invest in.

   Should you buy a Freehold or 99-year leasehold?

> Should you invest in the Core Central Region (CCR) or put your money in mass market districts?
>
> What kind of facing, floor level and layout should you go for?
>
> There are many other different considerations, in which the realtor should be able to advise you on the most suitable investment angle that can help you maximize the potential returns. Different angles work for different people; I do not think there is a one-size-fits-all solution that can be applied to anyone and everyone.
>
> If your realtor is unable to advice you, fret not. In Chapter 5 and 6, there are a total of 10 Secrets that you will learn – these 10 Secrets are my best kept strategies and tips that will not only help you to avoid making expensive mistakes with your property investments, but to also help you to achieve your desired profits and returns in the shortest time possible!

Once your realtor goes through the above 3 steps with you, then you will gain the final C – which is CONFIDENCE.

Confidence allows you to take swift and decisive actions with a clearer mind, because the opposite is always true – a mind filled with fear, disbelief and scepticism will always fail to make the right decisions.

I always share with investors that their investment is not just my responsibility, it is also a partnership between us. My goal is a win-win situation for both you and I, whereby you benefit from the investment returns while I benefit from the continued working relationship through the form of referrals and further collaborations in the future.

This is why I would only recommend properties that I am highly confident in about its investment potential and the expected returns... If I am not certain about any property, I will explain my rationale why, and it is then your call to decide if you would still want to proceed ahead.

In my early years in real estate, I've met several buyers who were hesitant just before they were about to proceed with the purchase. They already gained sufficient Clarity and Certainty, but lacked the Confidence to go ahead with the shortlisted investment unit.

When I asked them the reason for their hesitation, it's interesting how most of their answers were pretty similar:

"I can't believe it, it's happening too soon... Can I go back and think about it? I need to discuss with my _____ ..." (you can fill in the blank with your spouse / parents / children / friend, etc)

When I was less experienced, I would often let them go back to consider further...

Looking back, I shouldn't have done so.

When a buyer has last-minute concerns and fear, it is usually not that they disagree with the investment angle, nor is it that they have concerns about the property itself... Usually, the problem lies with the built-in defense mechanism in their minds.

You see, our brain is wired to protect us from making swift decisions. We are taught from young that making fast decisions is not good for us, because it would appear to be hasty and impulsive. The perception is that slower decisions would appear to be more "well-informed" and that sufficient time had been spent to think things through, therefore justifying the decision.

However, not every fast and swift decision made is necessarily bad. In the world of real estate, time literally can cost you more money! I've witnessed too many times when buyers missed out on their top choices just because of their last-minute hesitations, and ended up having to pay more for their less-preferred choices when their initial top choices were snapped up by other buyers.

So did I resolve this?

To instill the Confidence necessary to proceed, we need to look into what the facts and figures say.

Numbers don't lie; I rely heavily on what the numbers tell me to determine if the benefits outweigh the risks, and whether the property is indeed a sound investment to proceed with. Confidence is a natural consequence when you have studied the numbers and know what you are really investing your money in.

My preferred technique is to do 2 types of Comparative Analysis: Future-Based & Past-Based.

Future-Based comparison is basically relying on the price trends to forecast the future price growth, from which I can determine if there is sufficient price margin to leverage on for profits. It will be best if there are nearby empty land plots – even better if they are already listed on URA's website under the next batch of Government Land Sales due to be tendered for bidding.

Here's an example:

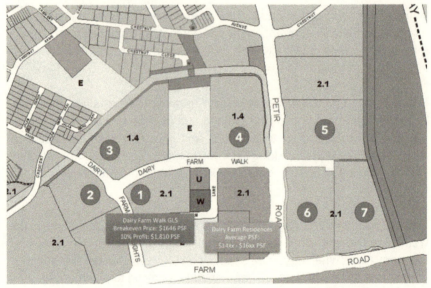

Source: URA

In the above illustration, look at Dairy Farm Residences. It is a mixed-development with both Residential and Commercial components, including its own supermarket, food court and retail shops. The development's average price was around $14xx - $16xx per square foot (PSF). There are an additional 7 plots of empty land that I've highlighted – these are all residential land plots due to be developed in the future, of which plot number 1 was sold on 11 March 2022 under the Government Land Sales tender.

Look at the breakeven cost of plot 1 – it is approximately $1646 PSF. Factor in a meagre gross 10% profit for the developer, and the selling price would have to be at least $1,810 PSF onwards!

Through this forward-looking method, we can deduce that buyers who purchased a unit at Dairy Farm Residences can expect a healthy profit in the future when they sell. That's how I sold units at Dairy Farm Residences to investors, and they took swift actions with Confidence because they understood what the numbers were telling them. With another 6 more plots of land yet to be sold, Dairy Farm Residences is in a good position to leverage on their future land sales, and this creates a safety net for their home owners to rely on.

My second method is Past-Based, which is to compare with past transactions and overall price trends of nearby developments.

However, when it comes to Past-Based comparisons, I do not just look at the PSF price trends. This is because older developments tend to be cheaper in terms of PSF anyway, as they were launched at lower prices last time. Instead of just focusing on PSF, I will also focus on the Price Quantum, which is basically the average price tags of transacted properties.

Now, do take note that normally newer developments tend to be higher in terms of PSF, so it is always challenging to do proper price comparisons between new and old developments.

This is why I will need to take additional factors into consideration, such as the properties' tenures, age of the properties, total number of units, total transactions sold in the past 12 months, as well as layout differences and also study the various facings.

Without taking the above factors into consideration, any direct price comparison between old and new would be rendered pointless, as most of the time price comparisons would favour older developments that are bigger in size and cheaper in price. I will go through this even more in-depth in Secret #17, from which you will learn why buying cheaper doesn't make you wealthier.

Here's a good Past-Based example: **Midtown Modern vs Duo Residences.**

These 2 developments are just right next to each other, located in the heart of Bugis. They are both mixed-developments, with retail shops on the ground floor. In fact, Duo Residences includes an integrated Grade A Office Tower, as well as an integrated hotel (which is Andaz by Hyatt). Both developments are 99-year leasehold, and the age gap is 8 years apart. Despite the 8 years' gap, Duo Residences' exterior façade was designed to be a timeless classic, with a futuristic look and design that wouldn't look out of place in a Star Wars scene.

If you just compare based on PSF alone, Duo Residences would appear to be the better choice, since it's so much cheaper than Midtown Modern.

However, we need to look even deeper before we can conclude if Duo is a better buy than Midtown Modern. Here's a direct comparison between Duo Residences' 2 Bedrooms and Midtown Modern's 2 Bedrooms, transacted in the same year on the same floor level.

Duo Residences 2 Bedrooms 936 sq ft 2021 Transacted Price: #20-XX $2.128 million ($2,273 PSF)	Midtown Modern 2 Bedrooms 721 sq ft 2021 Transacted Price: #20-xx $1.907 million ($2,645 PSF)

On paper, Duo Residences may appear to be the better deal. At 936 square feet (sqft), you seem to get a bigger unit on paper, at a much lower PSF of $2,273 PSF compared to Midtown Modern's 2 bedrooms at $2,645 PSF.

However, a closer scrutiny of the floor plans will reveal the uncomfortable truth – in Duo Residences' layout, you will find that there are inefficient spaces, such as the walkway between the rooms and the additional balcony in the common bedroom. Moreover, there is no additional room to be used as a store, which is what you get at Midtown Modern.

There is also no proper dining area in Duo Residences' 2 bedrooms, with an awkward space for a 4 seater table placed in the floor plan along the walkway to the hall. On the contrary, Midtown Modern's unit has a dedicated 6-seater dining area. Moreover, Midtown Modern's kitchen features a big C-shaped counter with a glass panel that makes the kitchen semi-enclosed, while Duo Residences' kitchen is a typical open concept dry kitchen.

In my personal opinion, the only positives I see in Duo's layout would be the slightly bigger bedrooms. Even so, it doesn't represent much more value for money. Although Duo Residences' PSF is lower, the Price Quantum is actually higher than Midtown Modern's unit by $221,000!

I personally wouldn't invest that extra $221,000 just for the bedroom sizes, because the additional space doesn't add much more functionality. But of course, that's my personal opinion.

Using this Past-Based technique, I can however deduce that resale buyers are willing to pay above $2.1million for a 2 bedroom unit in this location. Hence, for the buyer who bought The Midtown Modern unit, he or she should be able to see a healthy capital appreciation of at least $200,000 in the bare minimum. In fact, there are many others who bought as low as $1.7 million for the same layout, which means potentially even higher gains!

The expected rental rates would be in the range of $4,500 to $5,500, which means the gross yield is approximately 3.14% on average. Not too bad for a prime CCR district rental, as most typical CCR rental yields tend to be around 2.5% - 2.8%.

What I have just shared with you is a partial sample of my Past-Based method. As much as possible, I would combine both Future-Based and Past-Based comparative analysis to determine if a property is worth investing in, and it helps to give both myself and my investor clients more Confidence to proceed with the purchase. Ever since I developed this method of comparative analysis, my investor clients no longer needed to go back and reconsider just before proceeding with their investment.

You've now learnt what the 3 Cs are, and how to achieve all 3 Cs to ensure higher chances of success with your real estate investment. Well done to you!

Now, turn over to the next page, where I'll talk more about property bubbles. I think you're going to love this, see you in the next Secret!

Secret #10 – No One's Blowing Property Bubbles

"I'll wait till the property bubble bursts before I enter the market…"

That's one of the common statements I hear from investors, but is there truly a property bubble happening in Singapore?

A property bubble occurs when the market prices get inflated beyond economic principles and becomes unsustainable. Many years ago, the property market in Singapore nosedived at four different occasions between 1996 to 2009, due to the reasons stated in the chart below.

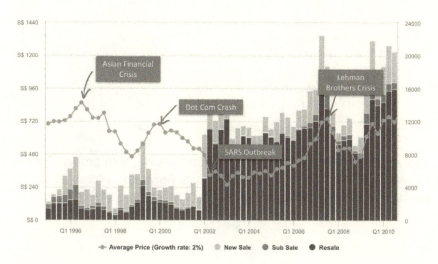

Source: EdgeProp, URA

As you can see, the real estate market in Singapore used to be vulnerable whenever a major crisis occurred – each of the four occasions above resulted in many people losing huge sums of money with their investments or business, and the overall growth of the market was negligible between the 13 years span from 1996 to 2009.

However, after the Lehman Brothers Crisis in 2009, Singapore's swift economic recovery started to attract global attention. How did a small island state with no natural resources manage to rebound so quickly? Foreign investors began to swarm into the country, investing billions into Singapore with high hopes and belief in the potential returns.

Based on the chart below, by the end of 2011 the total Inward Foreign Direct Investment (FDI) stock (money invested into Singapore) amounted to $672 Billion, while the Outward FDI stock (money invested out of Singapore) was $449 Billion. Observe how the investment figures rose exponentially higher towards the end, that was exactly the period of time when Singapore rebounded quickly from the Lehman Brothers Crisis.

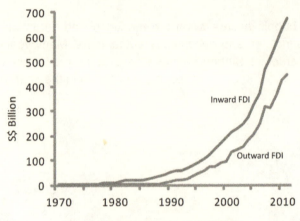

Source: Singapore Department Of Statistics

This also directly impacted the real estate market, with property prices escalating to new highs like never before. Between 2009 to 2013, the overall real estate price index went up by a staggering 147%!

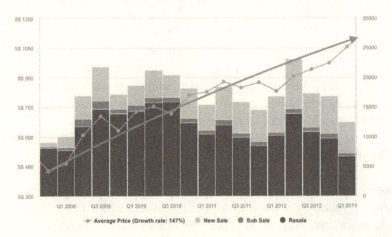

Source: EdgeProp, URA

Back then, the property market wasn't as tightly regulated by the government as what it is today. You could simply "flip and sell" to make quick profits within a matter of days by transferring the Option To Purchase to someone else for a higher price, and many people leveraged on the opportunity to make quick bucks everywhere.

Alas, Singapore's government loves closing the loopholes... in 2011, they amended the Seller's Stamp Duty to a 4 years period, which imposed a heavy restriction on individuals seeking to flip and sell properties upon acquiring them. For instance, if you sold the property within the first year, you would have had to pay 16% of stamp duty tax on the selling price.

Since 20 Feb 2010, the government started to implement cooling measures to cool down the property market. However, after 5 rounds of measures, the property prices remained on an upward trend with no signs of abating. Finally, on the th attempt at cooling down the market, the government succeeded.

The major measure that finally took the market down? It's called Total Debt Servicing Ratio (TDSR).

Introduced on 29th June 2013, this new measure changed Singapore's real estate landscape forever. A maximum of only 60% of an individual's monthly income can be considered for any housing loans, and the loan eligibility would be further reduced if you have any additional "debt" which includes car loans and credit loans. A separate loan framework, Mortgage Servicing Ratio (MSR) was also introduced specifically for HDB flats and new Executive Condominiums (EC, which factors only 30% of an individual's income for the housing loan.

(On 16 December 2021, TDSR was revised to factor in only 55% of an individual's average monthly income... a further reduction on loan eligibility).

The introduction of TDSR and MSR resulted in a huge reduction in people's borrowing power, which then caused both the private residential market and HDB market to tumble downwards. In the case of HDB, it was a downward spiral for more than 7 years, while the private residential market cooled down between 2013 to 2016.

Ever since then, the government succeeded in tightening their control over the property market, which prevented the possibilities of property bubbles thus far. There were many global incidents that threatened the real estate market to crash, such as Brexit, US-China Trade War, Covid-19 Pandemic, Russian-Ukraine War, and the global recession in 2022... Yet, real estate in Singapore stood against every single "test" and no bubbles were burst...

You can see that clearly in the chart below, which is the price trend of private non-landed residential properties from 2013 to 2022.

Source: EdgeProp, URA

Each time there was a major global issue that sparked concerns about real estate prices, the price simply continued to rise afterwards. This chart is a huge contrast to the earlier chart you saw, when global events used to have direct influence over our property prices.

Since 2016, we have not witnessed any property bubbles bursting, and now you know that it was a result of the government's tightened control of the real estate market.

The multiple rounds of cooling measures played a big part, but the key game changer was the introduction of TDSR and MSR. Not only did it limit borrowers' loan eligibility, it also meant that there are slim chances of over-leveraging from happening. Homeowners' holding power is now much stronger than ever before, and that also reduces the chances of them defaulting on their mortgage loans.

Clearly, the chances of property bubbles occurring is much lower than what it used to be, and now this should help to clear up any fear you have regarding any potential bubble bursts. However, the cooling measures are not the only mechanism helping to keep property prices in check... In the next Secret, I will reveal to you what most investors wished they knew sooner – the exact mechanism that allows you to plan your investment entry and exit strategies that makes your desired profits virtually guaranteed!

Go on, turn the page.

Secret #11 – Most Investors Regret Not Knowing This Sooner!

This Secret could just be the most important one that changes your view on Singapore's real estate forever. What I'm about to share with you is the key to many investors' success with their property investments, so pay close attention.

In the previous Secret, you've learnt that the government exerted greater control of the real estate market through many rounds of cooling measures, especially with the introduction of TDSR and MSR.

However, the extent of the Singapore government's control on real estate is far greater than you can imagine...

What if I tell you that the government is literally able to decide when to let the price go up and down?

In the most simple equation, the 2 key factors that affect property prices would be SUPPLY and DEMAND. When supply increases while demand goes down, it becomes an oversupply situation and prices would fall. When supply drops while demand surges, there is an under-supply and hence prices would rise.

While the government is not able to fully dictate the demand, they are however able to control the supply. After all, the government owns most of the land in Singapore, and they have the power to decide what to do with each plot of state-owned land. They decide how many Build-To-Order (BTO) Flats to build, and how many plots of land to be released for Government Land Sales (GLS) for developers to build private residential apartments.

Alright, so the government controls the supply. But how does that help in regulating real estate prices?

Once again, the answer lies in plain sight. If you study the real estate quarterly statistics published on URA's website as I've shared previously in Secret #8, you will find the relevant chart that tells you everything you need to know about the supply situation. Look for the chart that shows the **Pipeline Supply of Private Residential Units and Executive**

Condominiums by Expected Year of Completion via the e-services on URA Property Data's Download Statistics section.

For your benefit, I've combined the charts from older archives and the latest available statistic to illustrate the control of supply:

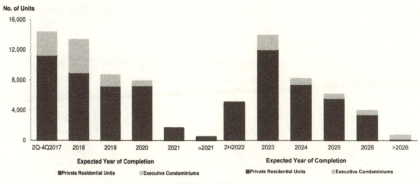

Source: URA

The above shows the private housing supply from 2017 to 2026 – the bars represent the amount of housing supply that is expected to be completed in that year. Do you notice a visible pattern with the supply?

Yes, the supply goes up and down in a visible cycle – the government allowed supply to increase for a few years, before decreasing the supply subsequently. If you study the chart, there was a huge surge of completed supply between 2017 to 2019, followed by a sharp drop after 2020 to 2021.

When there's a drop in supply, it meant that developers didn't have enough inventory in their land banks to run their business. This resulted in the massive en-bloc collective sale fever in 2017 and 2018, and that happened only because the government was not releasing sufficient land plots for sale...

Indeed, the government knowingly decided not to release too many GLS land. Henceforth, a total of $17.8 Billions worth of assets were acquired by private developers in response, which only halted when the government imposed higher taxes on developers on 6th July 2018, effectively warning developers that it was time to stop their acquisitions. Most of the new developments from the en-bloc fever were due to be completed in 2023 and 2024. After 2024, you will notice a steady decline in supply again...

which means that developers have to start accumulating inventory for their land banks again, and the cycle repeats once more.

Did you realise what you've just learnt?

By understanding how the government controls housing supply in such a predictable cycle, you can now plan and decide when to enter the market, and when to exit the market!!!

Now let's look at the chart below, in which I've added some visualizations for you to see more clearly how to time your investment.

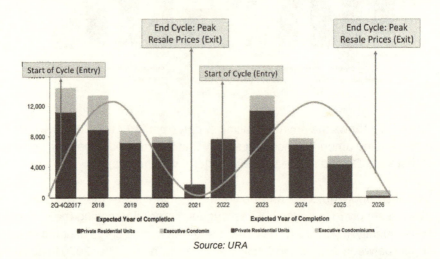

Source: URA

Looking back, those who entered the market in 2017 and 2018 could sell their properties by 2021 after waiting for more than 3 years in order to sell without incurring the Seller Stamp Duty (SSD). And guess what? In 2021 we witnessed a peak resale market, caused by the lack of supply. That was how many sellers generated high returns in that 3-4 year timeframe, by timing their exit accordingly with the cycle above!

Based on the illustrated chart above, the next low supply year would be in 2026. If you reverse engineer the 3 years SSD time-frame, the best time to enter would be between late 2022 to the end of 2023... and then you'll be able to sell the property in 2026 for the highest possible returns in another peak resale market.

Of course, all these are mere forecasts based on illustrated cycles, and no one can 100% guarantee your success. However, all this data helps us to maximise our potential returns, and minimise the risks at the same time.

All you have to do is to study this cycle, and I'm fairly certain that the government will always control the supply in such a predictable, cyclical manner. This way, you would be able to time your exit easily for any future real estate investments!

In this chapter, I believe you've gained more insights that help you to get the 3 Cs you need – Clarity, Certainty and Confidence, before you proceed with any real estate investments. This isn't the end though; in fact it's just the beginning.

What you've learnt is the general overview of Singapore's real estate market, and we are about to deep dive into more specifics in the following chapters. By going through the next few chapters, it should enlighten you even more on what you should invest in for yourself, and to also avoid unknown pitfalls that may cause you to suffer heavy losses.

Are you ready to learn more mind-blowing Secrets?

If yes, then let's go!

CHAPTER 4

WE NEED TO TALK ABOUT MONEY

Ever heard of the saying
"Money makes the world go round"?

Now, imagine if you could generate
more money out of thin air...

What would your world be like?

Secret #12 – Need More Money? Get It For Free

When we talk about getting money for free, most people would think it's impossible.

"There's no free lunch in this world!" they would exclaim.

"It must be a scam! Run!!!" that's probably what your friends would tell you.

In the world of real estate investments, however, there are ways to obtain money for free, so as to help you generate more funds to invest in the properties of your choice.

Let's take it as you are starting a business that you strongly believe in, but you don't have enough capital to start with. So what do you do? Instead of giving up on the idea, you can actually pitch to potential investors to invest in your business. In certain cases, we call these people "Angel Investors". There's a reason why they are seen as angels – with their injection of funds, they are the perfect support you need to kickstart a wonderful business idea, and turn it into reality. In return, these investors get ownership equity of the company and enjoy dividends from the business revenue as a shareholder.

You may argue that they are not doing it for free, as they are still earning some money from the business. The thing is, does the money come from you? No!

The money actually comes from your business' customers. You did not have to fork out a single cent of your own money to pay these investors! Your customers paid to buy your products or your services, and the income generated from there is then split into dividends to the angel investors, as well as your own share of the profits. Rightfully, as the business owner, you should still be the one earning the most.

Since the money paid to them doesn't come from your own pockets, you can therefore generate more wealth by using other people's wealth!

As an investor yourself, you need to learn and accept that sometimes, you cannot do everything by yourself. You need to **LEVERAGE**.

Majority of the world's top businesses leverage. They borrow huge sums of money from the bank, or get more cash injections from angel investors. Listed companies generate more wealth through selling their shares on the stock market, which is also a form of leverage.

When it comes to real estate investing, while it's uncommon to find angel investors to invest in your property purchase (unless it's your parents or close relatives), there is one big angel you can always turn to… and that's the bank.

You may think that I'm referring to the mortgage loan, but it's not exactly about that.

What I'm about to share with you, is how you can get more money from the bank even if you don't qualify to get the necessary loan amount!

That's right. We are going to ask the bank to give us more money to invest in a property, and you do not have to put a single cent in any fixed deposits with them (known as the Pledging method)!

Unknown to many, there is an alternative method, which is called "**Unpledging**". In layman terms, we call it the "show funds" method, which literally means you just have to show the bank that you have a certain amount of funds, and they will be willing to loan you even more money to help you afford the property you're keen on.

This is equivalent to you having to pitch your business ideas to angel investors – they need to know that it is safe to put their money with you, and the same theory applies with obtaining more money from the bank.

So how do we go about calculating this figure?

Firstly, you need to know how much loan is required for your property investment, and work out how much the income shortfall would be.

Let's work this out using a sample case study:

A couple, David and Debbie, are interested in buying a 2 bedroom condo for investment. The unit would cost them $1.5 million, and they require a 75% loan which would be $1.125 million.

David and Debbie, both aged 35, earn a fixed income of $4,000 each – that's a total of $8,000 combined income. For easy calculations, let's assume they currently do not own a car nor any credit loans. The loan amount they would be eligible for would only be approximately $980,000, which means they have a shortfall of around $145,000. How do they get this amount of money for free from the bank?

Let's use the Unpledging method, and here's the formula:

Income Shortfall x 48 / 0.3

The income shortfall is basically the difference between the required income to obtain the loan and the actual assessed income. In the above case study, David and Debbie's required income to obtain the full $1.125 million loan would be around $9,400 while the actual assessed income is $8,000.

So in this case, the income shortfall is $1,400.

As such, the unpledging amount required would be:
$1,400 x 48 / 0.3 = $224,000

The total amount of funds needed to be shown to the bank would be $224,000. This amount can be in the form of cash that is present in the bank accounts, and also class A shares equivalent invested with Singapore Stock Exchange (SGX). Equities in companies owned by the property purchasers may also be considered, subject to bank's approval. (Do check with a mortgage banker and seek proper advice, as each bank's requirements may vary.)

So now we know that if David and Debbie want to obtain a higher loan for free, they can show $224,000 worth of funds. The process only requires them to show the funds twice; once before signing the bank's letter of offer for the loan, and one more time just before the first loan disbursement.

This method would allow David and Debbie to also keep the $224,000 with them, serving as rainy-day funds or reserve funds to fall back on. Even though there will be loan interests incurred, it isn't going to be a substantial figure for most property investments. In fact, as long as they invest in an appreciating asset, it would be the next buyer paying off the interest for them! So the interests would eventually be fully covered by the sale of the property.

Imagine if they didn't know about this method to obtain a higher loan, they would only be able to invest in a property not more than $1.306 million – which would limit their investment options. They would have to either purchase a smaller sized unit or a unit in less desirable locations…

Of course, this method would only work if the purchaser has enough funds to show to the bank. That's why people say "money makes the world go round"… Being wealthy helps you to gain access to more means to become even wealthier, while those who don't have enough cash will be left with limited opportunities to grow their money.

This truth is further reflected in the form of mobile games and computer games, especially those that offer you means to upgrade your game character's skills and inventory items to progress further in the game, but you would have to pay for these upgrades.

These are known as "micro-transactions", and most of the time it would be extremely challenging to progress in the game without paying for the upgrades. If there is an online multiplayer mode, the winners of the game usually tend to be those who paid more for higher level upgrades.

Some people call this "Pay-To-Win" – and the same principle can be applied to real life… Every single day of our life, we are all playing the same game. The rule of the game is to live your life in the best manner possible, to achieve the most out of your time in this world, and live a fulfilling life that you can be truly proud of.

To win the game, you will need more money. You don't have to be the wealthiest, but you definitely cannot afford to be poor. As you accumulate your wealth, you will then be able to "unlock" more opportunities to multiply and scale your wealth to higher levels.

With some games, there would be free bonuses that aid you to get through the game more easily (in the form of free daily "loot boxes" or "daily log-in bonus"), and in the context of Singapore's real estate investments, the government does help to make it easier for you and I with their own version of bonuses too.

For Singaporeans and even Permanent Residents (PRs), the government assists us to grow our wealth through the Central Provident Fund (CPF), which helps to set aside a portion of your earned income for your retirement in the future. The CPF funds accumulated in the Ordinary Account (OA) can be used for housing payments. Hence, most local citizens and PRs heavily leverage on CPF funds for their housing investments, and that contributed to Singapore's high home-ownership rate of 91.7% (as of 2022).

However, while CPF funds are useful for most property investors and homebuyers, there are dangerous pitfalls with CPF funds usage, and I must share these with you. This could potentially affect your retirement plans, and I've witnessed people losing more than $100,000 and even over $200,000 in their CPF retirement savings, simply because they didn't know about the pitfalls.

Turn to the next page and I'll tell you more in the next Secret.

Secret #13 – Your CPF Money Is Not Always Yours

In the previous Secret, I shared about The Central Provident Fund (CPF), and it plays an essential role in helping many Singaporeans and Singapore Permanent Residents (PRs) to afford to buy real estate.

As of 2022, for those below 55 years old earning at least $750 a month, up to a total of 37% of the monthly salary gets credited into CPF accounts, which is further split into Ordinary Account (OA), Special Account (SA) and MediSave (which is used for healthcare payments). This becomes a form of forced savings for retirement, as the government's intention is to ensure that every citizen has the means to retire.

Only the funds in the Ordinary Account can be used for housing payments, which includes the down payments, stamp duties, loan instalments, and even legal conveyancing fees. For many, the usage of CPF funds helps a great deal, especially for those with minimal cash on hand. Without the forced savings in the CPF accounts, it's hard to imagine how many more homeless people we could see on the streets of Singapore...

With that being said, the use of CPF funds is not without its downsides. In the last 8 years, I've met and witnessed so many property owners who didn't fully understand the implications of using their CPF funds, and in many cases they even over-leveraged on CPF and ended up with huge losses eventually. Some even lost over $200,000 in retirement savings, and it was extremely painful for them to take.

So what caused these huge losses?

The answer is these two words: Accrued Interest.

As explained on the CPF board's official website:
Accrued Interest is the interest amount that you would have earned if your CPF savings had not been withdrawn for housing. The interest is computed on the CPF principal amount withdrawn for housing on a monthly basis (at the current CPF Ordinary Account interest rate) and compounded yearly.

Basically, CPF Board pays you 2.5% interest every year on the amount that still remains in your Ordinary Account, and as stated in the above statement, it is compounded yearly.

The crucial part is that the funds must remain in the Ordinary Account. If you had withdrawn them for housing purposes, the CPF board will not be paying you a single cent of the interest on the principal amount used! Instead, you now owe yourself the accrued interest, which must be refunded back into the Ordinary Account upon the sale of the property.

You may be wondering what's the fuss about, since you will still get the money back anyway after selling the property...

In the case of properties that have a positive capital appreciation which fully covers all accrued interest, there is absolutely nothing wrong. In fact, I strongly encourage investors and homebuyers to leverage on their CPF funds when the property's capital appreciation is highly certain. Upon selling with a positive profit, you get back all of the CPF funds used, as well as the accrued interest, and you can definitely use that sum of money to re-invest into the next property.

However, the major problem comes when the property ends up depreciating in price. If the selling price is not able to fully cover the total CPF funds to be refunded back into the Ordinary Account, there would then be a shortfall that rightfully has to be covered.

For example:
Edmund and Elaine sold their HDB flat above market value for $600,000.
Total outstanding loan = $350,000.
Total CPF used with accrued interests = $350,000.

Shortfall = $100,000

The above is a simple example of what we call "negative sale", whereby the sales price is unable to fully cover both the outstanding loan and outstanding CPF refunds. This scenario was extremely common between 2013 – 2019, when the HDB resale market declined for 7 years straight, and it also happens with condominium units that faced depreciation or long-term stagnation.

Thankfully, CPF Board has indicated that as long as the property is sold at market value (or close to, based on recent transactions and market valuation), there is no need to top up the shortfall incurred on the CPF refund. However, this also represents a loss on your end; the accrued interest was supposed to be your money that could have been in your CPF

OA for your retirement. What you lost isn't just the shortfall today, but it's also the compounded interest on the amount that could have been your money in the future.

For instance, with the above example, if the property sales price could fully cover the $350,000 CPF refund and earns the 2.5% compounded interest in the OA, in 10 years' time that $350,000 would grow to $448,029 without Edmund and Elaine doing anything. In contrast, by not covering the $100,000 shortfall, the refund of $250,000 into the OA from the property sale means that it would only grow to $320,021 in the same 10 years... that's $128,008 less than what it should have been.

What I'm trying to say here isn't that we shouldn't use CPF money. For most locals and PRs, CPF funds are almost indispensable, as the majority of the population doesn't have enough cash savings. Some would also prefer to put the cash aside for other forms of investments to yield higher returns than CPF's 2.5% per annum interest. That is also okay.

The more important thing you must grasp however, is that you should minimise the use of your CPF funds.

Through my observations, many people prefer to use their CPF funds to pay for the monthly mortgage instead of forking out cash. For those who are truly cash-strapped, it is unfortunately impossible to avoid using CPF funds... But there are people who do have sufficient cash reserves, and yet chose to fully utilise their CPF funds for a less-justifiable reason: why not use the CPF funds since it's money that we can't touch until we are at least 55 years old?

Just because you don't get to physically withdraw the money, doesn't mean you can abuse the use of that money.

By using CPF funds to pay for your mortgage payments, you are actually incurring double interests – the interest on the loan, and the accrued interest from CPF. This would contribute to more accrued interests which would continue to compound... Which increases the risks of facing negative sales in the future.

This is why I would strongly advise you to pay for your mortgage payments partially in cash, and use as little CPF as possible.

The worst that I've ever heard of, is a HDB owner who told me that he had fully paid off his HDB loans using his CPF funds, and he did so with a lump sum payment. Imagine the horror on my face when I heard that, while the HDB owner was beaming with pride that he had cleared off his loan and was supposedly "debt-free".

What he didn't realise was that he just trapped himself in a bigger black hole.

This was what he did. He bought a HDB flat for $500,000 and took a $300,000 loan from the bank. He also used $195,000 from his CPF OA, and used only $5,000 cash for the initial deposit. The monthly instalment (which was around $1200 per month) was also paid for using his CPF OA contributions, with no cash used.

After staying for about 7 years, he cleared the remaining loan with another $200,000 from his CPF OA. The loan was fully paid for, and he no longer had to pay a single cent of mortgage installments anymore. He then stayed for another 5 years, before deciding that it was time to sell his place to upgrade to another property.

Since the loan was fully paid for, there should be healthy sales proceeds, right?

But at that point of time, he wasn't aware of the implications with accrued interest…

In that 12 years, the total amount of CPF used with accrued interest was $563,803. His HDB flat's market valuation still remained at $500,000 – there was no growth as the flat was getting old, and the effect of lease decay meant that sooner or later the price would start to depreciate. So there was a shortfall of $63,803 at the very least… And by selling the flat, he would not be getting back a single cent of cash. Not even the initial $5,000 of cash that he used to buy the flat with.

By selling the flat, he would only get back $500,000 back into his CPF OA, instead of $563,803.

Not only would he lose at least $63,000 worth of funds in his CPF, he would also need to fork out more cash if he wants to purchase the next property!

The above scenario could be easily replicated with any property that doesn't appreciate in price. What I just did was to illustrate to you an example of the implications with CPF Accrued Interest, using a property that retained its market value with zero appreciation. Imagine if the property depreciated in price instead...

Now you might be thinking, in that case why not just hold on to the property and not sell it? After all, any loss will not be actual if the property isn't sold, right? Theoretically, yes. You don't lose anything if you don't sell. But it also means that the CPF funds will never go back to your CPF accounts for your retirement purposes, as all of the funds used are stuck with the property!

The use of CPF funds have helped many, but also harmed many. Some chose to put the blame on CPF Board, for imposing accrued interests on the principal amount used for housing. However, the real fault lies with people's ignorance about accrued interests, and also their own choice to over-leverage without proper knowledge of how to utilise their CPF funds more wisely.

Now that you know how CPF funds and accrued interests work, you should be in a better position than most to avoid making similar mistakes. Congratulations!

I think you should now be ready to proceed with the next Secret, in which you will learn a powerful secret that top investors use to dramatically increase investment returns. See you on the next page.

Secret #14 – How Smart Investors Don't Use Their Own Money To Be Rich

Have you ever wondered to yourself, how did someone get so rich?

Think about the Billionaires who made it without relying on inheritance money... Or major Multinational Companies (MNCs) raking in billions in revenue every year...

How did they even get started without having the capital to start with?

The answer is simple - they used other people's money!

In Secret #12 you learnt about how angel investors can help to fund a new business start-up, and how you can get more money from the bank to help you fund your property investment. Those are examples of how we can invest without using our own money, but even so there are still property buyers out there who are reluctant to take on "debts" to invest in real estate.

Most humans are wired to think that debts are bad, and they are constantly working to become "debt-free". But the smart ones know that there are bad debts, and also good debts.

Bad debts are situations whereby the borrower over-leveraged and stretched themselves beyond their means, with a misplaced confidence in their abilities to repay what they borrowed. It is also a bad debt when you are spending the money on a liability that doesn't bring you any positive cash flow.

Good debts, on the other hand, are healthy when you've done your due diligence and also give yourself sufficient breathing space to ensure that you can afford to repay the loans even if you lose your job or suffer from a reduced income. It is also a good debt when you are investing in an appreciating asset that provides healthy profits.

Now you might be thinking, why should I borrow money if I can afford to pay off the whole property in full cash? Why should I let the bank earn interest when I don't need any loans?

Well, if you can afford to buy a property in full cash, that is your choice to do so.

But when it comes to investing in real estate, we have to also consider the following two components: Return Of Investment (R.O.I) and Return Of Equity (R.O.E).

By buying a property in full cash, any potential returns would be considered as R.O.I, since the returns would be judged on the full amount paid for the property.

Let's assume that we are investing in a resale property worth $2 million paid in full cash, including the standard Buyer Stamp Duty for a local citizen - that would be an additional $64,600. So that's a total of $2,064,600 paid up front.

If this property appreciates by $400,000 in 5 years, assuming that there was no rental income, the R.O.I would have been calculated as such:

($400,000 / $2,064,600) x 100 = 19.37%
If divided by the 5 years' time frame, the R.O.I would be 3.87% per annum.

Now let's assume that instead of paying in full cash, we are going to take the maximum loan of 75% for the same $2 million property, at a fixed interest rate of 2.5% per annum for loan tenure of 25 years. The downpayment and Buyer Stamp Duty shall be paid for in cash:

25% Downpayment + Buyer Stamp Duty = $564,600
Average monthly interest payable @ 2.5 p.a. = $2,889
Total interest paid in 5 years = Approximately $173,340

With the same $400,000 appreciation, after deducting $173,340 of interest paid to the bank, there would still be a balance of $226,660 of profits. So now let's calculate the Return of Equity (R.O.E), which is basically the actual returns based on the amount of cash you've invested into the property.

($226,600 / $564,600) x 100 = 40.13%
Divided by 5 years' time frame, the R.O.E would be 8.026% per annum.

Compared to buying in full cash, the investment returns by taking a bank loan would actually be more than double!

You see, that's the advantage of leveraging other people's money through the housing loan from the bank. By doing so, you are also freeing yourself of approximately $1.4 million worth of cash (instead of putting them all into the property), which also allows you to either invest part of that money in other investment instruments, or to simply set aside as reserve funds for the rainy days!

Housing loans are one of the most essential tools for any property investor, and it is not just because it helps to increase your R.O.E. Unknown to many, the manner how housing loan payments are structured also benefits investors, by rewarding them with more profits the longer they hold on to the property!

This is all thanks to what is known as **AMORTIZATION.**

In layman terms, amortization basically helps to spread the total loan interest payable across the entire loan tenure, and the longer the loan tenure is the better it would be for you!

There are people with the misconception that they should borrow shorter loan tenure, simply because they cannot visualise themselves still "stuck with a debt" for 20 - 30 years. However, by shortening the loan tenure, that would actually increase the monthly instalment and also increase the amount of interest paid in a shorter time!

Moreover, loan amortization also means that your monthly interest actually reduces every month. The longer you hold the property, the less interest you pay!

The following table is a sample of an amortization table, of a $1.5 million loan for 25 years at 2% per annum:

Year 1 - 2.00%

Month	Interest	Principal	Total	Balance
1	$2,500.00	$3,857.82	$6,357.82	$1,496,142.18
2	$2,493.57	$3,864.24	$6,357.82	$1,492,277.94
3	$2,487.13	$3,870.69	$6,357.82	$1,488,407.25
4	$2,480.68	$3,877.14	$6,357.82	$1,484,530.12
5	$2,474.22	$3,883.60	$6,357.82	$1,480,646.52
6	$2,467.74	$3,890.07	$6,357.82	$1,476,756.45
7	$2,461.26	$3,896.55	$6,357.82	$1,472,859.90
8	$2,454.77	$3,903.05	$6,357.82	$1,468,956.85
9	$2,448.26	$3,909.55	$6,357.82	$1,465,047.29
10	$2,441.75	$3,916.07	$6,357.82	$1,461,131.22
11	$2,435.22	$3,922.60	$6,357.82	$1,457,208.63
12	$2,428.68	$3,929.13	$6,357.82	$1,453,279.49

Year 2 - 2.00%

Month	Interest	Principal	Total	Balance
1	$2,422.13	$3,935.68	$6,357.82	$1,449,343.81
2	$2,415.57	$3,942.24	$6,357.82	$1,445,401.57
3	$2,409.00	$3,948.81	$6,357.82	$1,441,452.76
4	$2,402.42	$3,955.39	$6,357.82	$1,437,497.36
5	$2,395.83	$3,961.99	$6,357.82	$1,433,535.38
6	$2,389.23	$3,968.59	$6,357.82	$1,429,566.79
7	$2,382.61	$3,975.20	$6,357.82	$1,425,591.58
8	$2,375.99	$3,981.83	$6,357.82	$1,421,609.75
9	$2,369.35	$3,988.47	$6,357.82	$1,417,621.29
10	$2,362.70	$3,995.11	$6,357.82	$1,413,626.18
11	$2,356.04	$4,001.77	$6,357.82	$1,409,624.40
12	$2,349.37	$4,008.44	$6,357.82	$1,405,615.96

Year 3 - 2.00%				
1	$2,342.69	$4,015.12	$6,357.82	$1,401,600.84
2	$2,336.00	$4,021.81	$6,357.82	$1,397,579.03
3	$2,329.30	$4,028.52	$6,357.82	$1,393,550.51
4	$2,322.58	$4,035.23	$6,357.82	$1,389,515.28
5	$2,315.86	$4,041.96	$6,357.82	$1,385,473.32
6	$2,309.12	$4,048.69	$6,357.82	$1,381,424.63
7	$2,302.37	$4,055.44	$6,357.82	$1,377,369.19
8	$2,295.62	$4,062.20	$6,357.82	$1,373,306.99
9	$2,288.84	$4,068.97	$6,357.82	$1,369,238.02
10	$2,282.06	$4,075.75	$6,357.82	$1,365,162.27
11	$2,275.27	$4,082.54	$6,357.82	$1,361,079.72
12	$2,268.47	$4,089.35	$6,357.82	$1,356,990.37

As shown, the monthly interest reduces every month. From $2,500 in the first month, it goes down to $2,268.47 by the end of the 3rd year.

So this also means that the longer you hold your property, the less interest you pay, which also represents higher returns if you are renting out your property! This is why older folks like to hold on to their properties for many years, because every single month they see more and more money coming to them instead of going to the banks.

That's why I would usually recommend investors to take more loans instead of using more CPF funds; by using CPF Funds, you are incurring accrued interest that compounds every year, while by taking a loan, you are leveraging on amortization that reduces your interest every month!

What I would suggest is to lower your CPF funds usage (I know it's almost impossible to use zero CPF for most people), and earn the 2.5% interest in the Ordinary Account from the CPF Board, and bite the bullet to pay a bit more cash for the loan installments. This way, you will receive more cash from the sales proceeds when you sell, and there would also be less stress on the property's selling price to cover your CPF refunds.

I know this may sound a little more painful since you would need to fork out more cash every month to pay off the loan, but I urge you to look at this as a form of **forced savings**. It would all be worthwhile when your investment yields your desired returns to help you achieve the life that you wanted!

In this entire chapter, you've learnt how investors use less of their own money to invest, and how you can leverage more on loans instead of your CPF funds to dramatically increase your R.O.E. I believe you are now much more ready to kickstart your real estate investment journey, but I wouldn't advise you to jump right in yet...

Turn over to the next chapter to learn some of the most costly mistakes that investors make unknowingly - I'm sure that you wouldn't want to suffer from the same mistakes!

CHAPTER 5

TOP 5 COSTLY MISTAKES MOST MAKE UNKNOWINGLY

The greatest mistake an investor can make is simply not learning from others' mistakes…

This could potentially save you from the heartache and pain of losing 6 to 7-figure from your property investment.

Secret #15 - The Ugly Truth About Public Housing

In Singapore, approximately 78% of the population resides in public housing built by the Housing Development Board (HDB), known as HDB flats.

To most, even though it's public housing, a HDB flat is considered one of their most important "investment" ever, with hundreds of thousands spent to acquire one. The sense of attachment is tied to both the sentiments of owning a home, and also the amount of money spent on the house...

I recall the days when I used to stay in a HDB flat with my family, and I fondly remember the huge kitchen, large bedrooms, and the convenience of having plenty of amenities right downstairs of my house. Even after my family upgraded to stay in a condominium, and eventually to a strata-landed terrace house, we would still reminisce about the HDB flat we used to stay in and talk about how much we missed the HDB flat we stayed in. If you've stayed in a HDB flat before, or if you're staying in one right now, perhaps you can relate to how we felt. Somehow, a HDB flat just hits differently, compared to private residential properties. It just seems to be more like... a home.

Maybe it is the community - the neighbours you meet on a regular basis, the aunties and uncles that say hi to you every now and then, the stall owners at the nearby coffeeshop who knows your food preferences inside out, and the friends you've made over the years in the neighbourhood.

For whatever reason it may be, many Singaporeans are attached to the idea of owning a HDB flat - there are even some old folks who still prefer to retire in a HDB after many years of staying in a private property. And this is where it gets dangerous - the sense of attachment to HDB tends to cloud people's judgments, causing them to make irrational decisions that may be very costly in the end.

If you are one of those who have strong emotional attachments to HDB flats, I hope you will not be offended by what I am about to share with you - my intention is to purely highlight the fundamental flaws and blind spots that many people overlooked, so that you can avoid making the same mistakes.

Now let's go back to the fundamentals of what public housing really represents - it's meant to be a low-cost, affordable housing option for the masses, not intended to be a tool of speculation or high investment returns.

For the younger generation who doesn't have much funds to kickstart their real estate journey with, going for a Build-To-Order (BTO) flat is the logical choice, as they can easily earn an average of $150,000 to $200,000 and more after selling their house upon the completion of the 5 years Minimum Occupation Period (MOP) required. The only slight downside is that these profits come at the expense of time - waiting for a BTO to be completed takes approximately 4 to 5 years, so it would take around 10 years to realise the first pot of gold from the sales proceeds.

While a BTO is generally safe and profitable, the time-consuming nature to realise the profits mean that it is not that suitable for older homebuyers. After all, time is also money, and the older you get the more precious time becomes.

However, the real danger lies in the HDB resale market - if you're not careful, you might end up being trapped in a poverty cycle that would adversely affect your ability to retire comfortably!

The reason why I would say so is because many Singaporeans enjoy taking grants from HDB to offset the purchase cost, without knowing how the grants would affect them adversely in the future. The common perception is that the grants from HDB are "free money", and there are even people who opted for the grants simply because they want to milk as much as they can from the government as a form of "revenge" for the taxes they pay to the government. *(Yes I know this may sound absurd, but I swear it's true - I heard this myself from a HDB buyer before.)*

Here is why you shouldn't take the grants from HDB, if you are thinking of going for a HDB resale flat: the grants are disbursed into your CPF Ordinary Account, and then withdrawn out from OA as part of the payment for the flat. If you recall back what you've learnt in Secret #13 about CPF, any amount used from your CPF OA for housing would incur the 2.5% compounding accrued interest from your property's sales proceeds...

So yes, by taking the grants you would also incur accrued interest on the grant amount received!

This would put more stress on the resale price to cover the full CPF refund - the more grants received, the higher the accrued interest it would be. The biggest irony is that the highest amount of CPF grants are given to those with the lowest income. While I acknowledge that it is out of good intention to help the poor to afford a home, it is also baffling that grants are disbursed via CPF instead of being a direct offset on the purchase price as a form of discount.

With the CPF accrued interest incurred on the grants received, while the grants may have helped the poor to have a shelter over their head, it may also continue to trap them in a poverty cycle that is hard to get out of.

Let me illustrate with an example - assuming a married couple David & Esther wants to purchase a HDB 4-room flat from the resale market as first-timer buyers, but their combined household income would be only $4,000 monthly. They decided to stay with their parents so that they would be eligible for the Proximity-Housing-Grant (PHG). Assuming that they chose to take the maximum eligible grants possible because it's "free money", here is how it would work out:

First-timer CPF Housing Grant for 4-room resale flat: $50,000
Enhanced CPF Housing Grant (EHG) for combined income $4,000: $50,000
Proximity Housing Grant for staying with parents: $30,000
Total grants eligible: $130,000

HDB Loan eligible with $4,000 income: approximately $239,000
Monthly instalment for 25 years loan @ 2.6% HDB loan interest: $1,084 per month

Assuming that David & Esther have only $50,000 CPF savings in the ordinary account and no cash savings to pay for the house, their maximum purchase price would work out to be around $400,000 after factoring in Buyer's Stamp Duty. Unfortunately, at $400,000 they would have extremely little options in the HDB resale market - most likely they would have to go for a much older resale flat with no appreciation value. (And we have yet to factor in renovation costs, but let's not continue to add on to the misery here...)

If they choose to use their CPF to pay for the monthly instalment every month, and stays in this HDB flat for 10 years before deciding to sell, this would be the amount of CPF with accrued interest to be refunded back into their OA:

Outstanding loan after 10 years: $161,468.22
Total CPF Refund including accrued interest: $376,148.81
Breakeven price = $161,482.22 + $376,148.81 = <u>$537,631.03</u>

As mentioned previously, with a maximum purchase budget of $400,000, it would be unlikely for them to be able to purchase a HDB flat with appreciation potential. More likely than not, the price would depreciate due to lease decay - or at most stagnate if they are lucky and could possibly sell it back at around the same price that they bought it for.

Even if they sell it back at $400,000 again, this would be a negative sales of more than $137,000 deficit… which interestingly works out to be almost the same amount of the grants they received. While they do not have to top up the deficit, the negative sales would also mean that they wouldn't receive a single cent of cash after selling the house.

While you may think that this isn't so bad after all since they had a house to stay in for that 10 years, the bigger problem is this: how are they going to afford their next housing?

For the same price of $400,000, the available housing options in 10 years' time would be even more limited than what it would be today. If they want to get another HDB flat, they are also unable to get as much grants as before since they are no longer first-timer applicants, and resale levy also applies if they get a second subsidised flat.

The only way David & Esther can afford to buy another house would be if their income had increased sufficiently, along with more CPF and cash savings. Otherwise, they would most likely conclude that it's better not to sell the property at all, and just hang on to it all the way… Which also means that all the CPF funds used for the house will never come back to their CPF Accounts for retirement, and their retirement funds are solely dependent on their personal savings or other forms of investments if any (chances are, there aren't).

Unfortunately, that is the ugly truth of public housing in Singapore - the poor remain trapped in the poverty cycle, and they have to rely on the government for more financial support. While it is definitely with kind intentions that HDB housing grants were introduced to help Singaporeans to afford a home, I personally think that it is an outdated policy to disburse the grants via CPF - in the past the accrued interests incurred could be easily covered by the HDB flat's appreciation, but in today's times the appreciation is less certain.

Again, it goes back to the basic fundamentals of public housing - it is meant to be affordable after all. One day the HDB resale price would be corrected downwards when the price hike is too much for most to afford, and that's when HDB sellers would feel the pain when their flat's value depreciates.

Hence, if you are unable to afford to invest in a private property and could only go for a HDB resale flat, then my advice would be to simply not take a single cent of grants from HDB. Don't fall into the same trap as many others did - there is no free lunch in this world, and the grants could just simply set you back even more many years down the road.

If you currently own a HDB flat and took some grants, then I would advise you to consider selling your flat if you have the means to upgrade to a private property. It just doesn't make sense to allow the accrued interest to continue eating into your sales proceeds, and it is just going to be harder for you to exit the longer you hold on to your HDB flat.

Perhaps now it is making more sense to you why there are increasingly more HDB owners upgrading to private condominiums - it is not just about making profits, but also to cut losses and avoid being trapped by the dangers of the CPF accrued interest. However, this doesn't mean that buying a private property would guarantee you success. That's why I've devoted the next 4 Secrets to share more with you about the mistakes made with private condo investments, so that you can take note of what to avoid for your own purchase.

Let's go on to the next Secret if you're ready!

Secret #16 – Why Buying Great Locations Don't Always Work

"Location, location, location… it's all about the location!"

That's the old cliche that we hear all the time when it comes to investing in real estate. But is it true that buying great locations would always be the most profitable?

The answer is a big NO.

I discovered this shocking truth while compiling research for my clients, and I must warn you first: what you are about to learn from this Secret could possibly change your perspective on real estate investments forever…

Before I continue, let me first put out a disclaimer: I am not saying that location doesn't matter, but it shouldn't become the main consideration for your property investment. There are so many more factors that contribute to a property's appreciation growth and rental demand; so even though location does play a big role, there are also massive blindspots that investors do not see simply because they were focusing too much on the location aspect.

The following case studies may shed more light and allow you to see why better locations may not necessarily be more profitable for investors:

La Fiesta vs Riversails

Both developments are located in District 19 and were also completed in the same year (2016), but with a distinctive difference - La Fiesta is located directly opposite Sengkang MRT Station, with a big shopping mall directly opposite and plenty of amenities nearby. On the contrary, Riversails is not near any train stations at all (not even the LRT), and there are not as many amenities in the surroundings as compared to La Fiesta. Both developments can be considered as high density, with more than 800 units each (although Riversails have 110 more units, it isn't a significant advantage over La Fiesta).

Source: OneMap

So the natural assumption would be that La Fiesta must be more profitable than Riversails because of the location, right? Well, the numbers don't lie. Let's look at the performance of both developments below:

Source: EdgeProp, URA

In the charts, you can see clearly that Riversails outperformed La Fiesta by 16%, despite being in a less desirable location. No doubt La Fiesta still commanded higher selling prices in the resale market, but the gap between both are increasingly narrow.

Is it because Riversails is a much nicer development than La Fiesta? Frankly, no. There's nothing much outstanding about Riversails - there aren't exceptional facilities or far superior layouts...

Some may argue that it's down to the entry price, as most buyers purchased Riversails as cheap as $800+ to $900+ per square foot (PSF), while La Fiesta's initial launch started at $1,181 PSF on average. The margins between the entry prices did allow Riversails to catch up further in the resale market, and initially I thought that must be the main reason that attributed to this weird phenomenon of Riversails outperforming La Fiesta...

That was until I researched further, and what I discovered was startling to say the least.

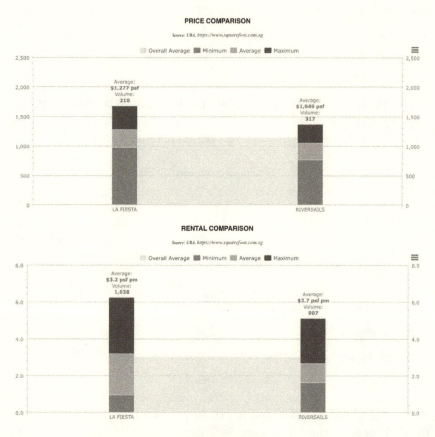

Source: EdgeProp, URA

In the bar charts above, these are the total resale and rental transactions since TOP in 2016. For the resale volumes, both are pretty much on par, with 210 transactions for La Fiesta and 317 transactions for Riversails. Considering that Riversails had 110 more units than La Fiesta to begin with, their transaction volumes can be considered as being on par with each other.

But once you look at the rental transactions, the disparity is clear. In La Fiesta, there were a total of 1,638 rental transactions compared to only 907 rental transactions at Riversails. That's a HUGE difference. You might think this is normal since La Fiesta is located in a better location, thus having higher rental volume, but I see a different picture.

Having so much more rental transactions at La Fiesta showed me a certain truth - there are more landlords in La Fiesta than in Riversails! Which means that more buyers purchased La Fiesta for investment purposes, while more purchased Riversails for own-stay. "Isn't it obvious? The better location is going to attract more investors of course!" - I assume that is what you are thinking in your mind.

All these may sound silly to you now, but I shall hold on to my punchline a little longer and move on to the next case study - you will understand my point better after I show you more. Wait for my punchline… wait for it. It's going to be worth it, I promise.

The Hillier vs Eco Sanctuary

Yet another classic example - both developments are located in District 23, completed in the same year (2016), and also have a very similar number of units (just 45 units' difference).

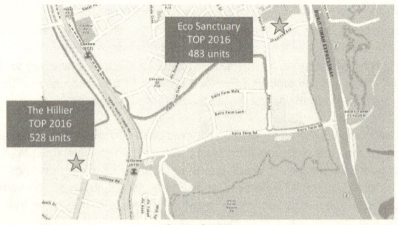

Source: OneMap

The Hillier is situated in the private enclave of Hillview estate, just 4 minutes' walk away from Hillview MRT station, it is also a mixed development with the shops at Hill V2 right below the residential units. On the contrary, Eco Sanctuary is not walkable to any train stations, it is surrounded by HDB flats, and there are no malls nearby (not even coffeeshops nor any eateries)... It's quite a contrasting difference to The Hillier, isn't it?

Now let's look at the resale performance of both developments:

Source: EdgeProp, URA

Once again, a wide disparity in the resale performance of both developments. The Hillier appreciated by 16% since its initial launch, although there are also a significant number of owners who bought at much higher prices and still could not realise their profits after 10 long years. Eco Sanctuary, on the other hand, appreciated by 34%, and we can be certain that pretty much most (if not all) of the buyers who bought from the early stages would have reaped healthy returns on their investment.

So what are the factors that led to the differences in their resale performance?

Well, entry price was once again a clear factor - and you can see how property buyers were so convinced by The Hillier's location that they deemed it was worth paying even over $1,600 PSF in 2013. As of 2022, the resale average is around $14xx PSF only. That clearly showed that buyers overpaid for The Hillier; even though it's common knowledge that better locations command higher premiums, in this case the premium wasn't justified.

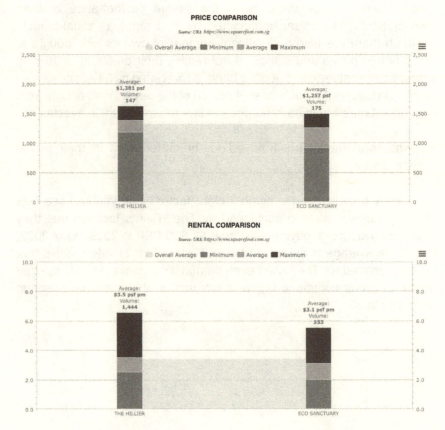

Source: EdgeProp, URA

Look at the total resale and rental volumes above since their completion in 2016 - do you notice similarities with the previous case study of La Fiesta versus Riversails?

The resale volumes of both developments are rather close, so we can assume that resale demand for The Hillier and Eco Sanctuary are on par. As for the rental transactions, The Hillier had a significantly higher rental transaction volume, once again a sign that there was a higher presence of landlords as compared to Eco Sanctuary... At this point, we need to start thinking about what this really means. Is it a problem when there are way more investors than home-stay buyers owning units in a development? Hmmm... I'll tell you more after showing you another case study from my research.

Vue 8 vs D'Nest

If you're familiar with Pasir Ris, you would know that the majority of the private condominiums are not exactly that near to the train station (with the exception of Pasir Ris 8) - the next nearest private developments would be either Coco Palms or D'Nest. It would take approximately 7 minutes to WALK to Pasir Ris MRT Station from D'Nest, while Vue 8 would also take the same 7 minutes to get there but by CAR instead. We can therefore be certain that D'Nest is in a much more favourable location than Vue 8.

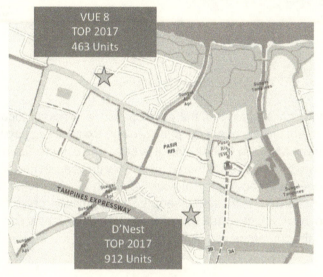

Source: OneMap

Being closer to the MRT station also means that residents at D'Nest enjoy closer proximity to amenities - they are closer to White Sands shopping mall and Pasir Ris Central Hawker Centre, while Vue 8 is nowhere near any major amenities of note.

Now let's look at the resale performance for both developments:

Source: EdgeProp, URA

Interestingly, once again it is the development in a poorer location that outperformed in terms of overall price growth. While D'Nest appreciated by an average of 26.9% since its initial launch, Vue 8 appreciated by 39%, despite having 449 less units than D'Nest. This proves that buying a better location does not necessarily provide you with higher profitability, and therefore unable to justify the higher premiums paid for "great locations". It also proves that bigger developments with "higher transaction volume" doesn't really guarantee you higher profits too.

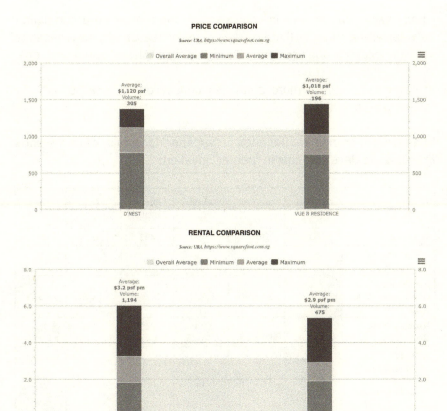

Source: EdgeProp, URA

Well, you should know the drill by now. Look at the resale performance; it is interesting to see that despite having way more units than Vue 8, D'Nest actually sold a smaller percentage of their development (D'Nest sold 33.44% of their development since TOP in 2017, while Vue 8 sold 42.33% in the same period of time). As for the rental volume, the higher presence of landlords is clearly evident in D'Nest too. With 1,194 transactions in 5 years, the average percentage of units rented out in D'Nest per year would be 26.18%, while for Vue 8 the rental transactions in the same 5 years represents only 20.5% of the development being rented out per year.

Don't you realise that in all 3 case studies that I've shared, they all showed very similar outcomes? The better the location, the higher the presence of investors and landlords, and in the end it's always the developments in poorer locations that performed better in the resale market, with higher transaction volumes and higher appreciation growth.

I personally don't believe in coincidence - there must be a correlation between all the statistics that would show us the reason why developments in better locations don't perform as well as those in less desired locations.

In order to achieve a more quantified conclusion, I came up with the following table below.

The boxes in orange are the ones in "superior" locations, while the ones in yellow are developments in "poorer" locations.

	La Fiesta	Riversails	The Hillier	Eco Sanctuary	D'Nest	Vue 8
Total Units	810	920	528	483	912	463
Resale Volume Since TOP	210	317	147	175	305	196
Percentage of Development Sold Since TOP	25.92%	34.45%	27.84%	36.2%	33.44%	42.33%
Rental Volume Since TOP	1,638 in 6 years	907 in 6 years	1,444 in 6 years	553 in 6 years	1,194 in 5 years	475 in 5 years
Average Percentage Of Development Rented Per Year Since TOP	33.7%	16.43%	45.58%	19.08%	26.18%	20.5%
Capital Appreciation Since TOP	19%	35%	16%	34%	26%	39%

Pardon me if you are not a "numbers person"; if the table above is too much for you to understand, then you just need to know my final conclusion from studying this table:

Developments in better locations tend to attract more investors, hence the higher rental volume. However, this also means that there would be less units for sale in the market, since the landlords are not selling their units! Moreover, even for own-stay owners, they are less likely to sell since the location has been so convenient for them. Therefore, this directly resulted in less resale transaction volume than developments in poorer locations, which impacted the capital appreciation growth.

Imagine paying a higher premium for a superior location, only to get less profits than those who invested in poorer locations...

I suppose at this point your mind would have been blown away by this surprising revelation, that great locations are not always the better buy. This is why you must not rely on common sense to invest in real estate; on the contrary, I discovered that reverse psychology usually works better for investors!

Location, location, location... It's important, but it's not everything.

See you on the next page.

Secret #17 - Buying Cheap Doesn't Make You Wealthier

"How To Spot <u>UNDERVALUED</u> Properties That Generates 6-Figure Capital Gains…"

Seen any online ads with similar headlines to the one above?

Many real estate agents like to use this word "Undervalued", to hook property buyers who are out to hunt for good deals. The reason why "Undervalued" works as a hook is because most people want to buy CHEAPER than what others are paying for, so it may seem like they got a better deal than others.

However, the funny thing about real estate is that cheaper prices do not always guarantee you profits, so if you don't finish reading this Secret you would probably suffer huge losses like many others did.

Perhaps most of us (including myself) are just too used to the common perception of a "good deal" - after all, on a day to day basis we find ourselves bargaining for cheaper prices in the groceries market, waiting for special dates like 11.11 to shop online for more discounts, or enjoying 1-for-1 drinks during Happy Hour in a bistro bar… Whatever that helps us to save money and get what we want at a cheaper price, that would represent "value for money" to most of us.

So it is no wonder that when it comes to investing in a property, many would apply the same thinking: if I am buying a property for cheaper PSF than what was transacted nearby, wouldn't it be a great deal?

Unfortunately, that is not always true.

Through thousands of hours spent on studying the real estate market, I discovered various reasons that caused investors to lose hundreds of thousands with their investment, and one of the most common reasons was simply the assumption that buying cheaper PSF wouldn't go wrong.

Here are some case studies from my research that shows clearly why you shouldn't buy a property just because it appears to be cheaper:

The Hyde vs Three Balmoral vs One Balmoral

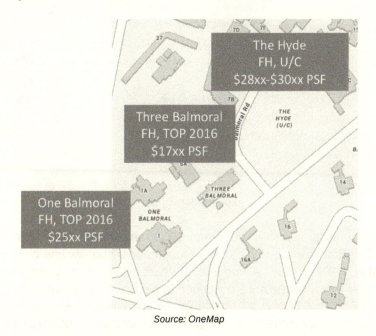

Source: OneMap

These 3 developments are right next to each other, located in prime District 10 along Balmoral Road. All three are Freehold developments, yet with very contrasting prices despite being in the same vicinity. As of today, their average price PSF is as stated above. One quick glance and you would assume that Three Balmoral can be considered as "undervalued", since it is the cheapest among these 3 projects right?

Well, this is what many years of being in real estate taught me: **cheap does not always mean value.**

Just because it is the cheapest doesn't mean it is the safest, and if you're not careful you could possibly be trapped with a property that doesn't see much appreciation growth for many years (yes, even if it's freehold)!

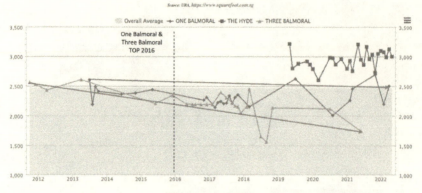

Source: EdgeProp, URA

Since the initial launch in 2012 and 2013 respectively, Three Balmoral and One Balmoral have yet to see much capital appreciation growth as of today in 2022. That's a long 9 to 10 years with minimal growth; in fact for Three Balmoral the price continued to dip downwards over time (from $2500 PSF to $17xx PSF!), while for One Balmoral there were some profitable sales, but the price growth was still not significant. If you bought One Balmoral on day 1 during the initial launch phase, after 9 years your sales proceeds may be barely sufficient just to cover all the loan interests you've paid.

Let's pretend that you invested in a unit at Three Balmoral in 2020 at above $2,000 PSF - back then it would have seemed like a very attractive deal, since The Hyde was selling at close to $3,000 PSF. What could go wrong? Well, the average price tumbled down to $17xx PSF just 1 year later... Looking at the overall price trends, there is no certainty that Three Balmoral could recover from its downwards spiral.

In fact, it's interesting to see that The Hyde continued to sell well at around $28xx - $30xx PSF on average, even though it was significantly priced higher than its immediate 2 neighbours. So why were buyers willing to pay so much more at The Hyde? Wouldn't it be better to go for the cheaper neighbours?

I studied these 3 projects intently, and discovered that the answer can be found in the floor plans...

The 3 examples above are all 3 bedroom types, and the highlighted areas in the floor plans of One Balmoral and Three Balmoral are what we call "wasted spaces" that are inefficient. It was a common feature in many developments built before 2016 - you would find plenty of bay windows and planter boxes that take up a lot of space in the gross floor area. Even though on paper the sizes appear reasonable for these 2 projects, you would notice that you could only fit in a single bed in both common rooms at One Balmoral, and the same goes for Bedroom 3 at Three Balmoral.

In comparison, although The Hyde's unit may seem much smaller at only 1,249 square feet, there are no wasted spaces in the layout, and every common bedroom can fit a queen size bed. Such is the efficiency of the layout that if you viewed all 3 properties in person, you would likely assume that all 3 layouts are about the same in size! This is extremely important when it comes to identifying developments to invest in - layout efficiency is one of the key factors that affect a unit's performance in the resale market. Little wonder why buyers are willing to invest more money into The Hyde - the layout is a clear winner compared to its "larger-sized" competitors next door.

Lesson learnt: look out for inefficient layouts - avoid wasted spaces at all cost!

Sky Vue vs Sky Habitat

Source: OneMap

If you've been to Bishan estate, you would not miss out seeing these 2 condo projects. Both are the only condominiums that are right next to Bishan MRT Interchange, and both developments look vastly different in terms of architecture design. Sky Vue looks just like any other typical condo, while Sky Habitat looks like it's an architecture masterpiece meant for the Ultra High Net-Worth (UHNW). Even in terms of facilities wise, Sky Habitat features more interesting facilities, including a roof-top lap pool on the 38th level! Interestingly, both projects were built by the same developer.

Source: EdgeProp, URA

Although both developments were completed just 1 year apart, the resale performance couldn't be more contrasting. As of today in 2022, Sky Vue's resale units fetched an average of $19xx PSF, while Sky Habitat remained stuck at $15xx PSF with very little appreciation since launch. Why is it that a typical-looking condo can outperform a luxury-lifestyle condo even though it's just right next to each other? Should you buy Sky Habitat even though it is currently cheaper by around $400 PSF?

Let's dive deeper to study these 2 projects.

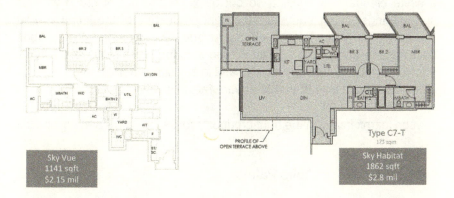

The above floor plans are the 3 Bedroom Premium types. Notice the huge disparity in the unit size? The 3 bedder at Sky Vue is only 1,141 square feet, while the same type at Sky Habitat is actually 1,862 square feet. In the previous case study, you already learnt about looking out for "wasted spaces", so I'm sure by now you would have noticed the HUGE Open Terrace at Sky Habitat's unit. This open terrace is literally an open-air terrace that is exposed to weather elements, with no shelter of any sort. It was deliberately done this way as part of the fanciful architecture design of Sky Habitat…

Take away the open terrace, and you would notice that there are no significantly bigger spaces in the Sky Habitat unit except for a larger dining area and slightly bigger kitchen.

Inefficient layout aside, the real problem here is this: would people buy a 1,862 square feet 3 bedder unit in Bishan estate??? The answer is likely a no.

That's because of one simple reason: Bishan is ultimately not a high-end prime estate. It is nothing like Orchard, Holland, Bukit Timah… So it is extremely baffling why the developer chose to build Sky Habitat as a high-end luxury condo in Bishan. It is a wrong product for the location, as the size is not something that mass market buyers can afford, while the concept of the whole development just feels off for Bishan as well. No doubt the architecture is iconic, but being iconic doesn't mean it would guarantee you profits.

Whenever I drive along the Central Expressway or around Bishan, the sight of Sky Habitat actually fills me with despondency... It is just like a white elephant, a building so out of place and out of touch with its surroundings. This clearly isn't the right product fit for the location, and the same theory can be applied to boutique developments with shoebox units in prime districts. In a location filled with affluent UHNW, does it make sense that there would be high demand to buy ultra small units like a studio apartment that's less than 400 square feet in size?

Lesson learnt: invest in the right product fit for its location's demographics!

NV Residences vs Coco Palms

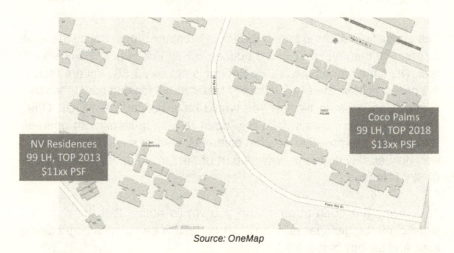

Source: OneMap

NV Residences and Coco Palms are located opposite of each other along Pasir Ris Drive, with a 5 years' age gap between them. However, despite being in the same location, their resale performances have been rather contrasting. One look at the chart below and you will be able to see that for NV Residences, their resale price dropped drastically since 2014, just 1 year after obtaining TOP, from its peak price of over $1200 PSF to as low as less than $900 PSF in 2018. It was only in 2021 that there was a significant price recovery, but the resale price was only back at the same levels as what it used to be pre-2014. This means that if you purchased NV Residences in 2014, after 9 years you would still be unable to sell for breakeven.

On the other hand, Coco Palms' price continued to rise upwards since its' TOP in 2018 from $12xx PSF to almost close to $14xx PSF today, with steady growth in the last 4 years. Even though NV Residences is clearly the cheaper option, Coco Palms appears to perform better in the resale market, and is likely to continue doing so. Why is it that the more expensive choice provides higher returns?

Source: EdgeProp, URA

The answer is simple: Singaporeans like to buy NEWER things.

Just look at how people change their mobile phones once every two years whenever their phone line contracts are due for renewal, or probably even change to the latest iPhone every year just to be using the latest model! Or to be rocking the latest sneakers, wearing the latest fashion statements, checking out the newest hotel for a staycation... The list goes on.

This is also why HDB buyers don't mind paying extra more money (probably at least $200k-$300k more) for a HDB flat that just completed its first 5 years' Minimum Occupation Period (MOP) - they like it that it's the newest HDB they can get in the market, and they can probably even save some money on renovation too since the existing renovation should still be able to last them for years to come.

The same theory applies to this case - Coco Palms, as the newest condominium around its location, attracts buyers who prefer to stay in a newer condominium, with nicer facilities and superior landscaping. Just look at the images of their respective facilities and the stark contrast is clear for all to see.

On the left is NV Residences, on the right is Coco Palms. NV Residences feature 5 small pools side by side, while Coco Palms has a mega-huge pool with a "mock beach" concept, along with floating platforms like the ones you see in the image above. It is not hard to see why Coco Palms commands a higher price than NV Residences in the resale market, and deservedly so.

Lesson learnt: Singaporeans like to buy newer things - including newer condos with nicer facilities!

Through the 3 examples above, I hope you now understand that a cheaper price tag shouldn't be the main consideration why you invest in a certain property. No doubt we all want to save some money on our investment, and it's normal to seek for "undervalued" properties… Now you know, cheap doesn't always represent value.

Also… What if I tell you that Freehold in prime locations isn't always safe too?

I'll leave that for you to learn more in the next Secret.

Secret #18 - The Greatest Lies Realtors Tell You About Freehold

Freehold vs 99-year Leasehold... The classic debate that never ends.

For the longest time, realtors have been telling buyers that 99-year leasehold properties are better than freehold. To some diehard fans of freehold properties, this may seem like a bitter pill to swallow. Is it really true though?

Well, if you look at what the overall data shows you on the surface, it may seem like these realtors got it right.

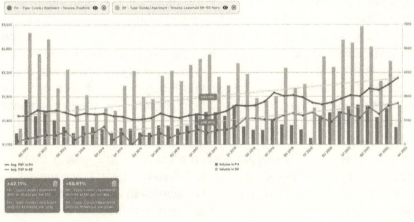

Source: Huttons, URA

The above charts showed that 99-year leasehold appreciated at a rate of 58.91% on average, while freehold appreciated by only 42.11% in the same 10 years' time frame. So does this mean that these realtors are telling the truth?

Unfortunately, NO. This graph only shows a glimpse of the truth, and yet it is being commonly used by realtors to convince buyers that 99-year leasehold properties are always going to be the more profitable option than freehold properties. When I was a new realtor, I was one of those who was so convinced by this graph, and started preaching to my clients about why they should buy a 99-year leasehold over freehold.

But as I became more experienced in this industry, and started to do more of my own homework, I realised that perhaps I was wrong after all. While it is STILL TRUE that some 99-year leasehold properties outperformed freehold properties, we cannot apply the same logic everywhere and assume that freehold is no longer a good choice for investment.

My revelation is actually very simple - there are freehold properties that are unprofitable, and there are also 99-year leasehold properties that are unprofitable. There are freehold properties that outperformed nearby 99-year leasehold properties, and there are also 99-year leasehold properties that outperformed nearby freehold properties... Do you see what I'm getting at?

You see, it's really NOT ABOUT 99-year leasehold versus freehold - what we should do instead is to identify the most suitable development for you to invest in. What I particularly dislike is that there are realtors who chose to show examples of freehold properties that were unprofitable, versus nearby 99-year leasehold properties that profited more, WITHOUT revealing the real truth behind. They would simply say "you see, this is proof that freehold isn't as safe as you thought", and then they would proceed to up-sell the 99-year leasehold property that they already had in mind to sell to you.

On the other hand, there are also realtors who are selling freehold properties, and they would say "this is definitely a good buy because it's freehold". After all, that isn't a difficult statement to accept because most buyers already have the perception that freehold is the safer choice... But that is also a dangerous assumption to make, because there are many other factors to consider before we can ascertain if the freehold property is indeed a good buy.

What I would suggest is to keep an open mind and look at properties objectively. Over the years, I've studied intensively into freehold properties, and developed my own framework of identifying common traits between profitable freehold homes and unprofitable ones.

To put it in a simpler analogy, I would look at freehold properties as if they are Rolex watches. For those who are unfamiliar with Rolex watches, they are considered one of the most highly sought-after watch brands in the world due to the way how their watches can retain value (and even appreciate) over time, similar to how freehold properties are perceived.

When it comes to Rolex, there are entry level watches such as the Datejust, and then there are the premium models such as the Daytona, Yacht-Master GMT II, and it also makes a difference with the appreciation of value depending on the rarity of the watch and its accessibility to be purchased. The basic concept is that entry level watches like the Datejust are much more affordable and accessible for the masses, but they do not appreciate as much in value over time due to lower demand (and generally higher supply). On the contrary, premium models like the Daytona are extremely hard to get in stores (and the waiting list for one is ridiculously long), so if you can get your hands on it you can certainly expect a potential 5-figure return on your purchase.

Now if we apply the same concept to freehold properties, then we can also categorise them into Entry-Level freehold and Premium freehold properties. Needless to say, premium freehold would be the more profitable choice.

Entry-Level Freehold

How do we define if a property is an entry-level freehold? Here are a few factors that can help us to identify them:

- Mass-market location *(Disclaimer: there are also entry level freehold in prime locations)*
- Boutique-development (less than 150 units)
- Compact layout / poorly-designed layout
- Poor aesthetics (architecture / facilities)

Of course, if a development has all 4 of the above attributes, it's definitely a no-go to invest in it. Now let's look at a few examples to better understand how entry-level freehold developments perform in the resale market.

Mass Market Freehold Example - Alexis

Located in Queenstown, Alexis is in a mass market location for sure. It is a well-known mature estate populated with mostly HDB flats, and the location doesn't exactly scream "high-end luxury"... You get it.

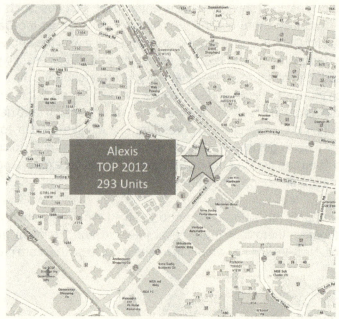

Source: OneMap

When we look at the resale performance of Alexis, it is clear and evident that even though it's a freehold property, it doesn't really inspire confidence in terms of its appreciation value. The resale price actually depreciated over a 10 years' period...

Source: EdgeProp, URA

Mass market boutique freehold example - Bijou

This mixed development with commercial shops is located directly opposite Pasir Panjang MRT station, and is just a short drive away from the Central Business District (CBD). It is also not situated in a HDB estate; instead, it is surrounded by an enclave of private properties, including landed houses. However, it is also directly facing the West Coast Highway, and is also opposite PSA's Pasir Panjang Terminal, a busy shipping port. Not exactly awe-inspiring even though it's freehold...

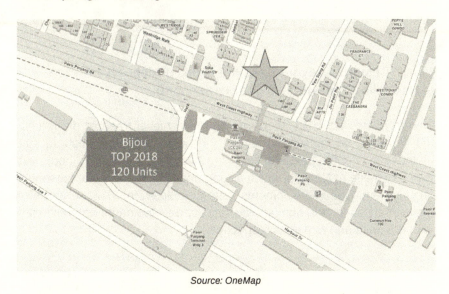

Source: OneMap

Even though Bijou is a freehold mixed development, the resale performance isn't very encouraging. Other than the fact that it is in a mass market location, it doesn't help that it is also a boutique development with only 120 units (realtors will spin it as "exclusive"), which further limits the transaction volume. Without sufficient resale demand, it would be challenging for Bijou's resale price to pick up significantly. As you can see, since Bijou obtained TOP in 2018, the resale price barely appreciated...

Source: EdgeProp, URA

Poorly-Designed Layout Example - Miro (Freehold) vs Rochelle At Newton (99-year Leasehold)

Even in prime district 11, there are also entry-level freehold properties, and Miro can be considered as one of them. To further illustrate that the location isn't the problem, I'm going to rope in Miro's neighbour next door - Rochelle At Newton, which also happens to be a 99-year leasehold development. Both developments were completed in 2012, so property age isn't an issue, and both are low density developments with not many units (85 units and 129 units respectively.)

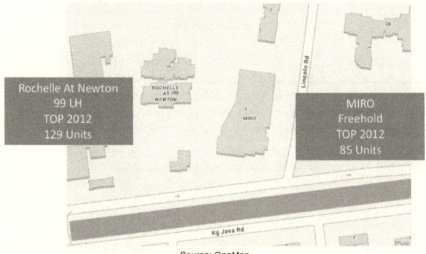

Source: OneMap

As we observe the resale performance of Miro and Rochelle At Newton, it is almost unbelievable - despite being a freehold development, Miro's resale price dipped by more than $600 psf after 2013, and the resale PSF was even surpassed by Rochelle At Newton in 2022. This shows that resale buyers are now willing to pay even more for a 99-year leasehold as compared to the freehold project next door!

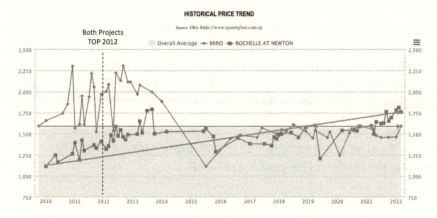

Source: EdgeProp, URA

From the chart above, we can even deduce that most of the first hand owners at Miro wouldn't be able to exit with profits even after more than a decade since they purchased their unit. So what contributed to the demise of Miro's resale performance? The answer can be found within the floor plan comparison below:

The above floor plans are both 3 bedroom types; on paper, it may seem like Miro has the bigger layout at 1,615 square feet, while Rochelle At Newton's unit seems to be slightly smaller. Upon closer scrutiny, you will realise that Miro's unit is actually a duplex (and it is the same for ALL of their units) - and there is plenty of void space as shown in the left side of the upper loft. Also, the kitchen in Miro is actually much smaller than that of Rochelle At Newton, not to mention that Miro's bedrooms are also smaller. Rochelle At Newton's master bedroom is significantly bigger, and the master bathroom even comes with a bathtub! There's even a study room within the master bedroom!

Product to product, it is clear that Miro's layout will be less appealing to most resale buyers. So what if it's freehold? In district 11, the wealthy buyers are looking to buy bigger and spacious layouts, and Miro is nothing near spacious despite being "bigger" on paper. Therefore, Miro falls under the entry-level freehold category even though it is in prime district 11.

Poor Aesthetics Example - Starlight Suites (Freehold) vs Martin Modern (99-year leasehold)

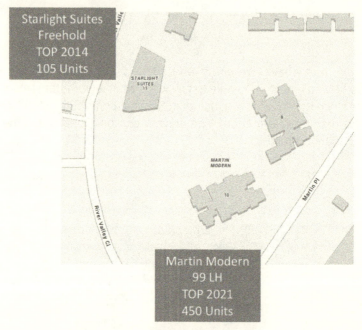

Source: OneMap

In another prime district example, Starlight Suites and Martin Modern are also right next to each other in district 9. Although there is a considerable age gap of 7 years apart, Starlight Suites is much cheaper than Martin Modern even though Martin Modern is a 99-year leasehold development. Both are directly opposite River Valley Primary School (highly regarded as a top school), and they are also within minutes' walk to the new Great World MRT Station.

Source: EdgeProp, URA

Looking at the resale performance, it is evident that Starlight Suites isn't that popular even though it's a freehold development in District 9. The average resale price of Starlight Suites in 2022 is even lower than that of its initial launch price in 2011! On the other hand, Martin Modern enjoyed a steady growth, and is priced at least $500 psf higher than Starlight Suites even though it is a 99-year leasehold development.

What is the cause of Starlight Suites' poor performance? One look at the following image and it would be clear to see:

The contrast between both developments couldn't be more clear from their mere appearance. Starlight Suites simply look like any other regular condominium, while Martin Modern exudes a classy, charming vibe that shouts "high-end luxury". The exterior facade and architecture does play a huge part in attracting resale buyers after all, as buyers are mostly emotionally-driven!

Although the saying goes "never judge a book by its cover", Starlight Suites is unfortunately like a book that would be left untouched on the shelf.

By now, you should be much more adept at identifying entry-level freehold developments to avoid! Congratulations! It is not that difficult isn't it?

In Secret #24, I will show you my proven strategies when it comes to selecting the right freehold property to invest in. But before we go that far, let's proceed to Secret #19 now on the next page. See you there.

Secret #19 - The Little Dirty Secrets Developers Didn't Tell You

Singaporeans love to invest in new launches, and it is no surprise to see many existing new launches being sold out even before they complete construction. However, not every new launch buyer gets to sell their unit for profit. How can you ensure that your new launch investment remains profitable?

To do that, you need to learn how developers think and work... And I'm about to let you in on the secrets that developers won't tell you.

The 30% Rule

What is the 30% Rule? Well, no matter how rich the developers are, they don't build a development using their own money. They would usually take a huge commercial loan from the bank to fund their construction costs, so that they can maintain a healthy cash flow to run their business.

However, the bank wouldn't lend developers the full sum right from the beginning... not until the development sold at least 30% of their units!

That's right. This acts as a form of security for the bank, to ensure that the developers are not building a development with extremely poor sales... hence the 30% rule. That's why for some new launches that take a while to hit the 30% mark, they wouldn't increase their prices so soon. There are likely good value deals to be discovered and invested in among the available units, so it would be worthwhile to explore these new launches that have yet to cross the 30% mark.

On a side note, this also means that for those new launches with more than 30% sold, the developers have already secured their full funding required to complete the development. This eases their pressure, hence giving them a stronger position to continue increasing the prices without having to give large discounts!

The Big Leap

Typically, most developers use the "dollar-averaging" strategy to price their units. What this means is that developers start off with lower prices to hook more buyers, hoping to hit the 30% mark as soon as possible, before increasing prices subsequently to achieve their desired profit goals.

However, it is also not wise to increase prices by too much within a short time; by doing so most buyers would be scared off by the dramatic price jump, which would likely result in a sudden dip in sales volume. That is why some developers tend to increase prices at a slower rate first even though they've achieved the 30% mark…

Once the sales figures hit the next milestone, the price would then take bigger leaps upwards when there is a strong sales momentum to maintain the price hikes. I call this "The Big Leap" - and it has been proven through many years of my research that the Big Leap is a common occurrence across various new launches. So at what point does the Big Leap happen?

Typically, the Big Leap happens when the total units sold fall around the 45% - 65% range or so (although there are also cases whereby it happens much later). Let's look at various examples and you will see clearly how developers increase price more dramatically from the Big Leap. For each illustrated example, you will see 2 charts - by studying both charts, you will be able to see approximately when the Big Leap happened, and how many percent of the development had been sold at that point of time.

The Florence Residences

The Big Leap: 52.9% Sold In June 2020

Source: EdgeProp, URA

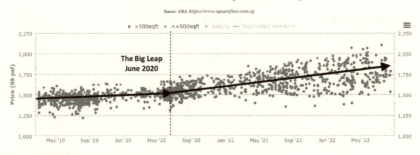

Source: EdgeProp, URA

Midwood

The Big Leap: 45.7% Sold In June 2021

Source: EdgeProp, URA

Source: EdgeProp, URA

Avenue South Residence

The Big Leap: 53.2% Sold In September 2020

Source: EdgeProp, URA

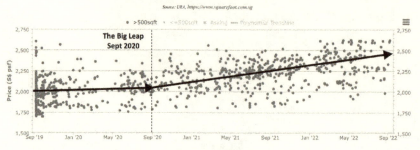

Source: EdgeProp, URA

Verdale

The Big Leap: 55.4% In September 2021

Source: EdgeProp, URA

Source: EdgeProp, URA

Artra

The Big Leap: 59% Sold In February 2018

Source: EdgeProp, URA

Source: EdgeProp, URA

In the above examples, you can see a significant leap in transacted prices after The Big Leap. As an investor, this is as good as finding the map to your desired treasure chest! Now you know about the 30% rule, and how developers execute The Big Leap. I'm certain that this knowledge will help you to avoid paying significantly higher than others for your real estate investment if you are going for a new launch project!

Believe it or not, the significance of knowing The Big Leap could potentially save you hundreds of thousands with your property purchase (not kidding)! Here's a real-life example for you to further understand how much money you could possibly save if you buy before The Big Leap.

#17-32
667SQFT
Bedrooms: 2
10 MAY 22
S$2,054PSF
S$1,371,000

#16-32
667SQFT
Bedrooms: 2
14 SEP 21
S$1,901PSF
S$1,269,000

#15-32
667SQFT
Bedrooms: 2
27 JUN 21
S$1,755PSF
S$1,171,000

#14-32
667SQFT
Bedrooms: 2
4 MAY 21
S$1,713PSF
S$1,143,000

#13-32
667SQFT
Bedrooms: 2
2 MAR 19
S$1,476PSF
S$985,000

#12-32
667SQFT
Bedrooms: 2
26 AUG 19
S$1,492PSF
S$996,000

Source: EdgeProp, URA

On the left, you will see a "Tower View" of the prices transacted for a development that I shall not name for obvious reasons. All of these units are of the same size, layout and facing as they are under the same stack.

In March 2019, #13-32 was sold for only $985,000. Just 3 years later the developer sold #17-32 for $1,371,000 - that's a huge difference of $386,000 for these two 667 square feet 2 bedder units that are just 4 floors apart! If you look at the transacted prices of the other units in between, you can also see significant price increments along the way.

That's the beauty of investing in new launches - investors love to leverage on developers' pricing strategies to gain an upper hand. Not only do you protect your future interests by getting a unit much cheaper than others, you can also exit sooner than the rest once you've fulfilled the waiting time to be exempted from paying Seller Stamp Duty (which is 3 years as at time of going to print).

So for #13-32, they could now sell their unit for at least $1.3 million based on the transaction of #17-32's price. That's a profit of more than $300,000 in just 3 years - and the capital outlay for #13-32 would have been only $270,400 if the buyer took a 75% loan. This is at least a 110% return on equity based on the $300,000 estimated profits (or 36.66% per annum)!!!

Meanwhile, #17-32 would have to wait till 2025 to sell, and any chances of profits would largely depend on whether the market valuation is able to support their desired asking price next time...

Do take note that the 30% rule and The Big Leap usually applies to new launches that take a longer while to sell - either in times when market is moving slower (either due to cooling measures or high supply of new launches), or when the development has too many units to sell (especially those with more than 800 units).

For those new launches that are sold more than 60%-80% on launch day, the developer could possibly increase price halfway during the launch, or days after the launch. Buyers who choose to take a "wait and see" approach may end up missing out completely due to the hot sales.

Be it a slow-moving project or a hot-selling one, if it is able to help you achieve your investment goals and objectives, you should take swift action before missing out on the best choice units. If you are unsure what are the criteria to look out for, go to **https://realestatesecrets.sg/bonus** to download a copy of my "Real Estate Investment Checklist" - it should serve as a useful quick guide to help you!

Are you still hungry for more knowledge? Because I still have many more Secrets to share with you… The next chapter is especially important, because I'm about to show you the exact investment strategies that helped many of my clients to achieve healthy 6 figure profits with their property investments!

The investment strategies await you on the next page…

CHAPTER 6

WHERE THE MONEY IS AND THE TOP 5 FASTEST WAYS TO GET IT

Investing in real estate doesn't have to be a gamble...

There are proven success stories that we can learn from, and actual investment strategies that you can follow...

Secret #20 - The Simple Way To Earn More While Spending Less

As an investor, I can be very certain that pretty much ALL of us want to earn more while spending less. Who doesn't?

However, many would think that this sounds too good to be true. After all, we were brought up with the saying "there's no free lunch in this world", and in true Singaporean context we also say "don't wait for durians to drop from the sky". In short, we were taught not to expect good things to come our way so easily.

Yet, every year there are thousands of investors who are using this simple way to spend less on their investment to maximise their returns. Even more shocking is that this simple way is actually not common knowledge to most; very often I've encountered investors and homebuyers who are not even aware of this method to help them save costs!

The simple way that I'm referring to, is to invest in a new launch property.

"Oh no, not again... Not another realtor who is trying to convince us to invest in a new launch!"

Wait a minute... Before you think that I'm just being a typical realtor, allow me to explain first.

When it comes to new launch properties, there is a unique function that you do not get with buying a resale property - and it is called "**Progressive Payment Scheme**" (PPS). Basically, what it means is that you would pay for the property in progressive stages according to the completed stages of construction, instead of having to pay the full sum upon the sales completion for resale properties.

For investors who decide to pay for the property in full cash, PPS grants the buyer more time to gather funds (usually from multiple sources) for the payment in stages. As for the majority of investors that obtain the maximum loan from banks, PPS also allows them to save significantly more money on loan interest!

Below is an example of a typical Progressive Payment schedule - we shall assume a purchase price of $2 Million with 75% loan at 2.5% interest for 25 years. This would be the payment schedule after you've paid the 20% downpayment and stamp duties:

	Estimated Period From Launch	Amount Disbursed by Cash / CPF	Loan Disbursed by Bank %	Amount Disbursed by Bank	Estimated Monthly Interest	Estimated Monthly Principal	Est Monthly Mortgage Repayment
10% FOUNDATION	6 MTHS	$100,000	5%	$100,000	$208	$240	$449
10% FRAMEWORK	6 MTHS	$0	10%	$200,000	$625	$721	$1,346
5% WALL	3 MTHS	$0	5%	$100,000	$833	$961	$1,794
5% CEILING	3 MTHS	$0	5%	$100,000	$1,042	$1,201	$2,243
5% DOOR & WINDOW	3 MTHS	$0	5%	$100,000	$1,250	$1,442	$2,692
5% CAR PARK	3 MTHS	$0	5%	$100,000	$1,458	$1,682	$3,140
25% TOP	12 MTHS	$0	25%	$500,000	$2,500	$2,883	$5,383
15% CSC	12 MTHS	$0	15%	$300,000	$3,125	$3,604	$6,729

One significant advantage of the PPS is the low monthly instalment figures. If you buy a resale property at the same price and exact same loan interest (actually resale interest rates are usually higher than new launch's interest, but for the sake of simplicity let's use the same interest rate here), the monthly instalment would be $6,729 from day 1, while for new launch you start paying only $449 per month ONLY after the foundation stage is completed. What a huge difference!

Typically for new launches, if you purchase a unit during the VIP Preview phase, it would usually take another 9 to 12 months before the developer completes the foundation stage for their construction. That means the bank loan would not be disbursed during those 9 to 12 months, hence the entire period is instalment-free for you!

For most investors, this is a significant game changer. Imagine not having to pay any loan interests for more than 9 months - that's a huge incentive for you. That's why for most investors, the strategy is to invest during the earliest phase of the new launch. Not only do you usually get the best price (and availability of course), you also get to buy before the foundation stage is completed. In 3 years' time you can then sell the unit for a healthy profit even before the development is completed (typically it takes 3 to 4 years to complete construction, subject to the development's targeted completion schedule). This is known as "sub-sale", and in such cases you wouldn't even have to pay a single cent of maintenance fees and property tax before the property is sold!

Now let's go back to the example mentioned above and compare the difference in average monthly interest paid to the bank in the first 3 years between a resale property and a new launch property (assumed to be purchased during preview phase):

Purchase Price: $2 Million
Resale average monthly interest @ 2.5% p.a interest: $2,988.83
New launch average monthly interest @ 2.5 p.a interest: $833

Resale estimated total interest paid in 36 months: $107,597.88
New launch estimated total interest paid in 36 months: $29,988
Total interest difference in 36 months: $77,609.88

More than $77,000 saved on loan interests paid - that's how investors spend less to earn more. Not only do they spend less on loan interests, they also do not have to worry about finding the right tenants that would take care of the house, nor to pay for any repairs / rectification works.

Looking at the past 5 years' trends, we would also observe an increasing demand for new launch properties, with higher transaction volume year after year since 2018 (there was a dip between 2017 and 2018 due to a drop in supply, before the en-bloc fever in 2018 increased the housing supply dramatically).

Year	Total New Launch Units Sold
2017	9,713
2018	8,060
2019	8,863
2020	9,488
2021	13,198

Is it a mere coincidence that demand for new launches is rising? Or is it because the buyers know how PPS can help them to spend less and earn more?

Nobody knows for sure, but we can be certain that PPS is indeed able to help you save significant sums on your total outlay on your property investment. If you're a pure investor seeking to maximise your gains and returns, you may want to consider investing in a new launch property soon.

Secret #21 - Big Ways To Big Profits

I once had an investor client, Mr Yong (not real name) who was fixated on investing in a landed property for pure investment. Mr Yong previously invested in a resale condominium, but there wasn't much profit even though it was a rather cheap property in a good location. Afterwhich, he bought a landed home, and in just 3 years he reaped almost $1 million in return. As I analysed his landed investment, I couldn't help but marvel at his perfect entry and exit timing (that he wasn't even aware of).

He entered the market in late 2018, and sold the property in early 2022. If you remember the market cycle that I shared in Secret #11, in 2018 it was a market with high supply, and in 2022 it was a low supply situation. The nearly $1 million return on his landed investment was almost timed to perfection, and thus it made perfect sense for him to re-enter into the landed property market again... But there was one issue.

Mr Yong's specific requirement to me was this: in his own words, he wanted to invest in the "fastest horse" that could give him the best results in the shortest time, and to also spend the least to maximise his returns at the same time. Right away I knew in my mind that investing in a landed property wasn't going to be the "fastest horse". In actual fact, there are plenty of "hidden costs" involved in purchasing and maintaining a landed property (such as pest control, waterproofing, gardening and more), not to mention the hefty renovation costs involved if it's an old landed property. As this was supposed to be a pure investment venture, Mr Yong wouldn't spend over the odds for newly renovated or rebuilt landed homes either.

Prior to meeting me, Mr Yong's idea was to invest in a landed property with land size of around 2,500 square feet, and would be happy if it could yield him a healthy return of approximately $700,000 or more in the next 3 to 4 years. After I shared my research and insights with him, I then proposed one of my proven investment strategies, which is to invest in **BIG SIZED UNITS**. Instead of investing his money in a landed property of 2,500 square feet land size, I proposed to invest in 2 units of private condominiums that add up to around 2,500 square feet in built up area, with him investing in 1 unit and his wife investing in the other (thankfully her name wasn't tied to any other properties).

Why invest in big sized units?

When it comes to new launch properties, most investors tend to put their money in the smaller unit types, be it the studio apartments, 1 bedders or 2 bedders... Yet I think otherwise. If affordability isn't an issue, I would recommend to invest in a bigger sized unit instead because the following reasons:

- Bigger sizes mean higher returns - a $250 PSF on a 1,000 sq ft unit is already $250,000.
- Higher demands for big units (just think of HDB flats - more people buy the bigger types such as 4-room, 5-room flats instead of 3-room flats. Same theory applies for condos as most resale buyers are buying for own-stay with their family members.)

So here was my proposed strategy to Mr Yong:

Invest in 2 units
1 x 1,100+ sqft 3 bedder
1 x 1,300+ sqft 4 bedder

To hit the required target of $700,000 in profit, we would require an average appreciation growth of $291 PSF for both units, which is perfectly achievable for most new launches.

PROFITABLE TRANSACTIONS
(TOTAL OF 36 TRANSACTIONS)

Note: Transactions with the same address are matched. Profitability of each round-trip transaction is based only on the change in asset price and does not take into account transaction costs and the effect of financing.
Source: URA, https://www.squarefoot.com.sg

SOLD ON	ADDRESS	UNIT AREA (SQFT)	SALE PRICE (S$ PSF)	BOUGHT ON	PURCHASE PRICE (S$ PSF)	PROFIT (S$)	HOLDING PERIOD (DAYS)	ANNUALISED (%)
18 NOV 2021	91 WEST COAST VALE #XX-02	1,518	1,614	12 JUN 2018	1,305	469,000	1,255	6.4
6 AUG 2021	91 WEST COAST VALE #XX-02	1,518	1,634	5 MAY 2018	1,329	463,000	1,189	6.5
11 AUG 2021	91 WEST COAST VALE #XX-02	1,518	1,693	12 JUN 2018	1,405	437,000	1,156	6.1
14 SEP 2021	91 WEST COAST VALE #XX-02	1,518	1,523	12 JUN 2018	1,246	420,000	1,190	6.3
17 DEC 2021	91 WEST COAST VALE #XX-06	1,249	1,554	12 JUN 2018	1,266	359,000	1,284	6.0
18 JAN 2022	91 WEST COAST VALE #XX-06	1,249	1,558	12 JUN 2018	1,272	357,000	1,316	5.8
15 SEP 2021	93 WEST COAST VALE #XX-15	1,066	1,717	5 MAY 2018	1,396	342,000	1,229	6.3
11 OCT 2021	91 WEST COAST VALE #XX-06	1,249	1,578	7 JUN 2018	1,309	336,000	1,222	5.7
30 AUG 2021	91 WEST COAST VALE #XX-05	1,141	1,516	5 MAY 2018	1,234	322,000	1,213	6.4
27 DEC 2021	91 WEST COAST VALE #XX-05	1,141	1,578	5 MAY 2018	1,307	309,000	1,332	5.3
15 NOV 2021	93 WEST COAST VALE #XX-15	1,066	1,699	5 MAY 2018	1,410	307,000	1,290	5.4
19 OCT 2021	91 WEST COAST VALE #XX-06	1,249	1,666	5 MAY 2018	1,420	307,000	1,263	4.7
17 DEC 2021	93 WEST COAST VALE #XX-15	1,066	1,614	5 MAY 2018	1,330	303,000	1,322	5.5
30 AUG 2021	91 WEST COAST VALE #XX-05	1,141	1,534	6 MAY 2018	1,289	279,000	1,212	5.4
27 AUG 2021	93 WEST COAST VALE #XX-15	1,066	1,530	5 MAY 2018	1,279	267,000	1,210	5.5
10 SEP 2021	93 WEST COAST VALE #XX-10	1,055	1,505	5 MAY 2018	1,257	262,000	1,224	5.5
30 NOV 2021	91 WEST COAST VALE #XX-05	1,141	1,507	5 MAY 2018	1,288	250,000	1,305	4.5
4 OCT 2021	93 WEST COAST VALE #XX-10	1,055	1,536	6 MAY 2018	1,300	249,000	1,248	5.0
27 SEP 2021	93 WEST COAST VALE #XX-10	1,055	1,498	5 MAY 2018	1,262	249,000	1,241	5.2
15 OCT 2021	93 WEST COAST VALE #XX-10	1,055	1,593	5 MAY 2018	1,380	224,000	1,259	4.2

Source: EdgeProp, URA

For instance, Twin VEW, one of the newest developments in West Coast with no accessible train stations nearby, achieved a healthy appreciation rate of around $250 to $300 PSF on average. Look at the highest profit - $469,000 achieved in a span of 3 years and 5 months - and that was a 1,518 square feet unit that appreciated by $309 PSF. This is proof that you don't need the most prime locations to make money with real estate, and the appreciation growth is indeed possible for bigger units to achieve our desired results.

Source: URA, https://www.squarefoot.com.sg

SOLD ON	ADDRESS	UNIT AREA (SQFT)	SALE PRICE (S$ PSF)	BOUGHT ON	PURCHASE PRICE (S$ PSF)	PROFIT (S$)	HOLDING PERIOD (DAYS)	ANNUALISED (%)
6 APR 2021	93 PRINCE CHARLES CRESCENT #XX-06	1,195	2,017	15 JUN 2016	1,536	575,000	1,756	5.8
22 FEB 2021	93 PRINCE CHARLES CRESCENT #XX-06	1,195	1,949	17 JUL 2016	1,516	509,888	1,681	5.5
4 JAN 2021	93 PRINCE CHARLES CRESCENT #XX-06	1,195	1,848	31 OCT 2015	1,491	426,000	1,892	4.2
25 SEP 2020	97 PRINCE CHARLES CRESCENT #XX-17	1,238	1,970	8 NOV 2015	1,629	421,000	1,783	4.0
23 OCT 2020	97 PRINCE CHARLES CRESCENT #XX-17	1,238	2,003	31 OCT 2015	1,669	414,000	1,819	3.7
25 JAN 2021	97 PRINCE CHARLES CRESCENT #XX-22	1,076	1,997	31 OCT 2015	1,666	357,000	1,913	3.5
29 JUL 2020	97 PRINCE CHARLES CRESCENT #XX-22	1,076	1,904	31 OCT 2015	1,625	301,000	1,733	3.4

Source: EdgeProp, URA

The above example is Principal Gardens - the top profitable unit is a mere 1,195 square feet unit that appreciated $481 PSF in slightly less than 5 years and generated $575,000 of profit. The other profitable units also show healthy appreciation of over $300 PSF and more.

In Secret #20, we learnt that it is possible to leverage on new launches to lower the capital outlay and pay less to earn more, so for Mr Yong he quickly understood how investing in 2 big units with new launch properties could yield him higher returns while paying less.

While I understand that not every investor has the affordability to go for big sized units, my investment strategy is still straightforward - invest in the **"maximum size based on maximum price"**! Go for the biggest possible unit that you can get with what you are able to comfortably afford, and it should reap you healthy rewards as long as the property also meets the other criteria that I've set out for you in the "Real Estate Investment Checklist".

If you still haven't got a copy of that yet, go to the following link and get yourself a copy now:
https://realestatesecrets.sg/bonus

Secret #22 - Know What The Rich Really Wants

When it comes to investing in prime luxury properties, this is where many investors got their hands burnt. Often we would see news articles reporting of units in the Core Central Region (CCR) losing millions, and the comments on social media never fail to mention how it was a big waste of money to invest in prime areas.

I once had a client, Mr Jay (not real name) who wanted to invest in a particular new launch project in District 10; he had no prior experience in real estate investments, but he was keen to own a piece of prime real estate. I shall not name the project, but what he had his eyes on was an exclusive freehold development in Stevens area, with an attractive location and posh design. Yet I told Mr Jay to avoid investing in this new launch, even though it appears to be a great deal on the surface. He was puzzled. Why would I say no to a prime freehold development in District 10?

My answer to him was simple - the rich and wealthy wouldn't be interested in this development at all.

Even though it was located in a prime district, within walking distance to the train station and also within 1 kilometre to Anglo-Chinese School (which is a big plus point to most buyers), the major problem lies with the size of the units. The 3 bedroom type in the project was only 915 sq ft in size, and a 2 bedroom premium ranged from 657 sq ft to 721 sq ft. While the sizes may seem pretty common among most new launches, it is not the right size to attract wealthy buyers in the resale market.

Think about this. If you're a rich multi-millionaire with lots of cash to burn, would you settle for a 915 sq ft unit to stay with your family? The clear-cut answer is no. Yet I've witnessed so many investors making this dangerous mistake of investing in prime luxury properties that aren't the right size and layout for its intended market. Instead of attracting wealthy buyers, small layouts tend to attract those who can't afford spacious high-end properties, thereby limiting the potential price growth.

My rationale is straightforward: don't buy a mass market product in a prime luxury location (and the same applies for the opposite!).

If you come across any new launches in prime districts, the first question you must ask yourself is this - does the size and layout feel like what wealthy people would stay in? If the answer is no, then simply avoid the project and move on to others. It may be your lifelong dream to own a property in the CCR, but if it is not the right product fit for the marketplace, it would not be the right investment for you.

Look at the following case study of **The Rise @ Oxley:**

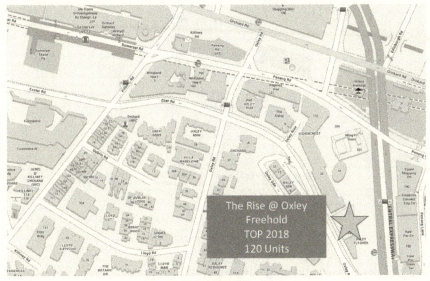

Source: OneMap

The Rise @ Oxley is a mixed development in prime District 9 that is just minutes walk' away from Somerset MRT Station, and interestingly is also located within close proximity to where the late Mr Lee Kuan Yew once lived in at Oxley Garden. However, its location, freehold status and proximity to the former residence of Singapore's most influential man ever are not enough to prevent a lack of price growth since its launch in 2014.

Source: EdgeProp, URA

PROFITABLE TRANSACTIONS
(TOTAL OF 2 TRANSACTIONS)

Note: Transactions with the same address are matched. Profitability of each round-trip transaction is based only on the change in asset price and does not take into account transaction costs and the effect of financing.
Source: URA, https://www.squarefoot.com.sg

SOLD ON	ADDRESS	UNIT AREA (SQFT)	SALE PRICE (S$ PSF)	BOUGHT ON	PURCHASE PRICE (S$ PSF)	PROFIT (S$)	HOLDING PERIOD (DAYS)	ANNUALISED (%)
1 JUN 2022	73 OXLEY RISE #XX-09	463	2,420	23 JUN 2014	2,333	40,000	2,900	0.5
21 OCT 2021	73 OXLEY RISE #XX-09	463	2,377	19 JUN 2014	2,312	29,999	2,681	0.4

UNPROFITABLE TRANSACTIONS
(TOTAL OF 3 TRANSACTIONS)

Note: Transactions with the same address are matched. Profitability of each round-trip transaction is based only on the change in asset price and does not take into account transaction costs and the effect of financing.
Source: URA, https://www.squarefoot.com.sg

SOLD ON	ADDRESS	UNIT AREA (SQFT)	SALE PRICE (S$ PSF)	BOUGHT ON	PURCHASE PRICE (S$ PSF)	PROFIT (S$)	HOLDING PERIOD (DAYS)	ANNUALISED (%)
14 APR 2022	73 OXLEY RISE #XX-01	1,163	2,032	5 JUN 2016	2,108	-88,000	2,139	-0.6
18 OCT 2021	73 OXLEY RISE #XX-09	463	2,161	23 JUN 2014	2,340	-83,100	2,674	-1.1
31 MAY 2021	73 OXLEY RISE #XX-08	818	2,139	29 SEP 2014	2,261	-99,677	2,436	-0.8

Source: EdgeProp, URA

Despite the total of 120 units, there were only 5 resale transactions since the development was completed in 2018 - 2 profitable ones (with the highest profit at only $40,000) and 3 unprofitable transactions just a few hundreds short of $100,000 lost. Most of them purchased their units in 2014, and they decided to cut their losses after holding on for at least 6 to 7 years without any significant returns.

Of course, in Secret #18 you already know about entry-level freehold properties, and The Rise @ Oxley certainly falls within that category even though it's located in the heart of District 9. Simply put, no matter how good the price may be, do not invest in an entry-level product in areas where the rich and wealthy reside!

If your intention is to generate 7-figure profits from investing in the prime estates, it is not impossible. All you need to do is to identify the right products that affluent buyers would be attracted to. Here's a more recent case study whereby several investors made more than $1 million in profits within a short span of time by investing in what the rich really wants:

New Futura

Source: OneMap

Completed in 2017, New Futura only started public sales of their units in 2018 - a bold but smart strategy by the developer (none other than City Developments Pte Ltd aka CDL) that paid off handsomely. Not only did it build up the hype around the project, the sales launch was also perfectly timed as 2018 was a year of strong demand for housing due to the en-bloc fever, where plenty of en-bloc millionaires were out hunting for new homes in the market.

It is also no coincidence that among all the districts in Singapore, District 9 and District 10 has the highest value of en-bloc collective sales done with more than $22 Billion worth of properties acquired by private developers in the last 20 years. Therefore in 2018 there was a surge in demand from en-bloc millionaires within District 9 and 10 to find their next replacement home, and New Futura benefited from that by launching their sales during then. Freehold in District 9, ready to move in immediately, and even featuring a Sky Gym designed by Porsche... Even at an average price of around $3500 PSF to $3800 PSF, buyers snapped up the units very quickly.

In just 3 years since then, we witnessed 7-figure profit gains at New Futura.

SOLD ON	ADDRESS	UNIT AREA (SQFT)	SALE PRICE (S$ PSF)	BOUGHT ON	PURCHASE PRICE (S$ PSF)	PROFIT (S$)
13 JUL 2021	18 LEONIE HILL ROAD #XX-05	2,250	3,956	8 FEB 2018	3,211	1,675,800
14 JUN 2021	16 LEONIE HILL ROAD #XX-02	2,691	4,088	25 MAY 2018	3,410	1,824,200

Source: EdgeProp, URA

These 2 units were purchased at lower than average entry prices, from $3211 PSF to $3410 PSF. The profit gained was $1.675 million and $1.824 million respectively, in just 3 years' time. Now look at the size of the unit, they are both above 2,000 sq ft in size. What does that tell us?

Yes, what the rich want is SPACE. Plenty of space. They don't mind spending and giving you 7-figure profits if they can get what they want - an ultra-premium freehold development with large space. New Futura is far from being an entry-level freehold property; it's one of the best freehold developments in District 9 and the rich buyers know it. The thing is, such properties are not affordable for most people, and it is truly a rich men's game. That's how the rich become richer by leveraging prime real estate to generate wealth.

So if you are thinking of investing in prime districts to gain such a high 7-figure profit, you need to have deep pockets to begin with. It is a high entry barrier no doubt, and that's exactly the point. To qualify for the rich men's game, you have to be rich enough first. If you can afford it, then congratulations - you could possibly be one of these owners with 7-figure profit from your investment! But if you're not qualified to afford such properties, then I would strongly advise against investing in District 9 and District 10. We have to admit it when we are not in the same league as those ultra-rich. Don't invest in entry-level developments in these districts - it's not worth your money, time, and energy.

So what should you invest in then?

The answer is in the next Secret.

Secret #23 - The Evergreen Demand You Can Always Rely On

In the last Secret, you learnt that investing in prime districts is a game for the ultra-rich - so what do we invest in if we aren't at the same income level?

Very simple - we invest in the mass market. What I'm counting on is the evergreen demand - which means that there will always be demand from mass market buyers. You have HDB Upgraders, or young families who want to stay in private properties, or even retirees who want to enjoy their retirement in a smaller condo after selling their landed houses... It's a wide spectrum of potential buyers for mass market condominiums.

Besides, the numbers also make more sense for developments in the heartlands.

For example, between investing in a 2 bedder of 700 square feet in the city versus investing in a 3 bedder of 1,000 square feet in the heartlands area, if both are at the same price without a doubt I would go for the 3 bedder in the heartlands. This is because real estate investment isn't just about the location; it's also about the potential returns based on the invested capital.

Let's work out the numbers for more clarity:

700 sqft 2 bedder in town versus 1,000 sqft 3 bedder in heartland
Assuming Purchase price Is The Same: $2 million ($2,857 PSF for 2 bedder, $2,000 PSF for 3 bedder)
Total downpayment + stamp duties required: $564,600 Cash + CPF

If I want a return of minimum $250,000 for a 44% return on equity, this would be the PSF growth required on the 2 properties:

700 sqft 2 bedder - $357 PSF growth required
1,000 sqft 3 bedder - $250 PSF growth required

With a bigger sized unit, there is less pressure on the appreciation growth, as only $250 PSF growth would already be sufficient to hit our targeted profits. I don't need to sweat on the appreciation, and neither do I need to worry about the potential demand. While it may be true that in the city there is a higher potential for more capital appreciation, the pool of potential buyers for the 2 bedders in the city would still be smaller than that of a 3 bedders in the heartlands.

Interestingly, even a 2 bedder in the mass market districts would still outperform those in the city. Remember what I said about spending less and earning more? This couldn't be more evident when you look at the results of **Commonwealth Towers** below.

PROFITABLE TRANSACTIONS
(TOTAL OF 125 TRANSACTIONS)

Note: Transactions with the same address are matched. Profitability of such round-trip transaction is based only on the change in asset price and does not take into account transaction costs and the effect of financing.
Source: URA, https://www.squarefoot.com.sg

SOLD ON	ADDRESS	UNIT AREA (SQFT)	SALE PRICE (S$ PSF)	BOUGHT ON	PURCHASE PRICE (S$ PSF)	PROFIT (S$)	HOLDING PERIOD (DAYS)	ANNUALISED (%)
14 MAR 2022	230 COMMONWEALTH AVENUE #XX-04	1,076	1,942	13 APR 2017	1,503	472,400	1,796	5.3
29 SEP 2021	230 COMMONWEALTH AVENUE #XX-04	1,076	1,914	28 JAN 2017	1,528	415,500	1,705	4.9
6 OCT 2021	232 COMMONWEALTH AVENUE #XX-19	1,302	1,981	20 SEP 2017	1,704	360,000	1,477	3.8
31 MAY 2021	230 COMMONWEALTH AVENUE #XX-04	1,076	1,877	30 MAR 2017	1,553	349,388	1,523	4.7
1 JUN 2018	230 COMMONWEALTH AVENUE #XX-07	689	1,880	30 MAY 2014	1,379	345,300	1,463	8.0
7 SEP 2021	232 COMMONWEALTH AVENUE #XX-15	1,055	1,967	19 AUG 2017	1,646	339,200	1,480	4.5
31 MAY 2018	230 COMMONWEALTH AVENUE #XX-07	689	2,003	22 MAY 2014	1,515	336,300	1,470	7.2
7 FEB 2022	230 COMMONWEALTH AVENUE #XX-04	1,076	1,979	25 JUL 2017	1,680	322,000	1,658	3.7
29 JUN 2021	230 COMMONWEALTH AVENUE #XX-07	689	1,887	27 MAY 2014	1,424	319,000	2,590	4.0
27 JAN 2022	232 COMMONWEALTH AVENUE #XX-21	904	1,953	12 APR 2017	1,601	318,300	1,751	4.2
18 DEC 2018	230 COMMONWEALTH AVENUE #XX-07	689	1,902	22 MAY 2014	1,441	317,200	1,671	6.2
5 NOV 2021	232 COMMONWEALTH AVENUE #XX-21	904	2,002	22 APR 2017	1,652	316,100	1,658	4.3
17 MAR 2022	232 COMMONWEALTH AVENUE #XX-15	1,055	1,915	9 AUG 2017	1,616	315,200	1,681	3.8
19 AUG 2021	232 COMMONWEALTH AVENUE #XX-19	1,302	1,766	8 APR 2017	1,526	312,000	1,594	3.4
21 AUG 2020	230 COMMONWEALTH AVENUE #XX-07	689	1,878	27 MAY 2014	1,430	309,100	2,278	4.5
30 DEC 2019	230 COMMONWEALTH AVENUE #XX-07	689	1,844	28 MAY 2014	1,396	308,600	2,042	5.1
2 JUL 2021	232 COMMONWEALTH AVENUE #XX-21	904	1,913	1 APR 2017	1,573	307,400	1,553	4.7
5 MAY 2021	230 COMMONWEALTH AVENUE #XX-10	904	1,920	9 NOV 2016	1,582	305,200	1,638	4.4
29 APR 2021	232 COMMONWEALTH AVENUE #XX-21	904	1,858	31 MAR 2017	1,528	298,400	1,490	4.9
23 OCT 2019	230 COMMONWEALTH AVENUE #XX-07	689	1,887	23 MAY 2014	1,470	287,600	1,979	4.7

« ‹ Page 1 of 7 › » 20

Source: EdgeProp, URA

Notice the units that are 689 sq ft in size - there are many units that achieved more than $300,000 profits within a span of 4 years on average. The 3 bedders in Commonwealth Towers (the 1,076 sq ft units at the top of the list) also achieved more than $400,000 profit within 4 to 5 years, a very healthy return for a real estate investment. Why are they able to gain so much profit? I am sure you know the answer by now - it's the evergreen demand from the mass market. Located in Queenstown, one of the most well known mature estates in Singapore, there is a high demand for private residential properties, and those who invested in Commonwealth Towers were able to reap significant returns from their investment.

To further illustrate my point about evergreen demand, let's study the results at **The Tapestry**, located along Tampines Avenue 10 (which is far from any train station).

PROFITABLE TRANSACTIONS
(TOTAL OF 43 TRANSACTIONS)

Note: Transactions with the same address are matched. Profitability of each round-trip transaction is based only on the change in asset price and does not take into account transaction costs and the effect of financing.
Source: URA, https://www.squarefoot.com.sg

SOLD ON	ADDRESS	UNIT AREA (SQFT)	SALE PRICE (S$ PSF)	BOUGHT ON	PURCHASE PRICE (S$ PSF)	PROFIT (S$)	HOLDING PERIOD (DAYS)	ANNUALISED (%)
25 JAN 2022	55 TAMPINES STREET 86 #XX-24	1,485	1,427	19 MAY 2018	1,171	380,800	1,347	5.5
12 APR 2022	57 TAMPINES STREET 86 #XX-28	1,432	1,453	13 OCT 2018	1,200	361,990	1,277	5.6
22 APR 2022	57 TAMPINES STREET 86 #XX-28	1,432	1,446	14 JAN 2019	1,210	337,340	1,194	5.6
25 AUG 2021	57 TAMPINES STREET 86 #XX-27	1,615	1,313	24 MAR 2018	1,106	334,400	1,250	5.1
30 SEP 2021	57 TAMPINES STREET 86 #XX-27	1,432	1,398	24 MAR 2018	1,189	299,400	1,286	4.7
14 JUN 2022	51 TAMPINES STREET 86 #XX-04	743	1,595	16 NOV 2020	1,260	249,450	575	16.2
20 OCT 2021	53 TAMPINES STREET 86 #XX-19	990	1,540	24 MAR 2018	1,289	248,200	1,306	5.1
16 AUG 2021	53 TAMPINES STREET 86 #XX-15	1,130	1,478	24 MAR 2018	1,265	240,400	1,241	4.7
27 OCT 2021	53 TAMPINES STREET 86 #XX-19	990	1,585	27 APR 2018	1,346	237,550	1,279	4.8
25 MAY 2022	55 TAMPINES STREET 86 #XX-22	926	1,566	3 APR 2018	1,314	233,380	1,513	4.3
30 SEP 2021	63 TAMPINES STREET 86 #XX-55	700	1,687	24 MAR 2018	1,361	228,000	1,286	6.3
27 SEP 2021	53 TAMPINES STREET 86 #XX-19	990	1,515	26 MAR 2018	1,340	173,220	1,281	3.6
26 NOV 2021	55 TAMPINES STREET 86 #XX-22	926	1,491	20 APR 2018	1,308	169,050	1,316	3.7
23 OCT 2018	61 TAMPINES STREET 86 #XX-38	474	1,797	24 MAR 2018	1,451	164,110	213	44.3
30 SEP 2021	59 TAMPINES STREET 86 #XX-33	700	1,644	24 MAR 2018	1,432	148,400	1,286	4.0
15 SEP 2022	53 TAMPINES STREET 86 #XX-17	689	1,582	23 MAY 2018	1,384	136,400	1,576	3.1
20 SEP 2021	57 TAMPINES STREET 86 #XX-28	1,432	1,299	8 JUN 2018	1,205	135,510	1,200	2.3
2 JUN 2021	59 TAMPINES STREET 86 #XX-34	700	1,558	24 MAR 2018	1,373	129,200	1,166	4.0
14 JUN 2021	63 TAMPINES STREET 86 #XX-56	990	1,414	15 APR 2018	1,296	116,960	1,156	2.8
29 AUG 2022	59 TAMPINES STREET 86 #XX-33	700	1,608	24 MAR 2018	1,449	111,400	1,619	2.4

Source: EdgeProp, URA

Remember in Secret #21 where I shared about the "Big Ways To Big Profits"? At The Tapestry, you can see that the big sized units are the ones with highest profits, with those above 1,400 sq ft in size (which are 4 bedrooms units) grossing over $300,000 in profit within 4 years. While not as impressive as Commonwealth Towers' results (which is clearly because Tampines isn't as attractive as Queenstown estate), it is still proof that evergreen demand can work in your favour in mass market locations. Even with a minor growth of only slightly above $200 PSF in appreciation, the 4 bedrooms units at The Tapestry were able to earn the owners more than $300,000 profit due to the unit size.

The cost of buying the 4 bedrooms at The Tapestry from the developer in 2018 was only around $1.7 million on average - which was around the same cost of a 2 bedder in the city that is not more than 700 sq ft in size. That means to achieve the same profits, the city 2 bedder would have to appreciate more than $400 PSF - hardly an easy task.

I am a firm believer that the mass market holds great power over the real estate market - it is the bottom-line that pushes the whole market forward. With new launches in the OCR (Outside of Central Region) already crossing the $2,000 PSF mark in 2022, I foresee that it will continue to drive resale prices upwards, and those who do not invest early enough will soon be left behind to rue their missed opportunities.

Secret #24 - The Reverse Psychology Method That Worked Wonders

One of the most classic debates in real estate would be about "Freehold Versus 99-year Leasehold". While I've already covered some examples of how you shouldn't invest in entry-level freehold developments, I've also stated that we shouldn't rule out freehold properties completely - and in the same manner we shouldn't rule out 99-year leasehold properties either.

Instead, what we can do is to use a Reverse Psychology method:

In a location mostly populated by 99-year Leasehold properties, buy Freehold.

In a location mostly populated by Freehold properties, buy 99-year Leasehold.

While this may sound a little gimmicky to you, I'll share with you real life case studies of how this reverse psychology method has worked well for many other property investors.

Buy 99-year Leasehold Surrounded By Freehold

Common sense would say that in a location where majority of the properties are freehold estates, it would be illogical to invest in a 99-year leasehold. This would be especially true for certain districts such as District 9, 10 and 15, where there is an abundance of freehold properties for buyers to choose from.

"I'd be crazy to buy a 99-year leasehold when there's so many freehold properties to choose from!" that would probably be what a freehold die-hard fan would say.

Yet it has been proven that the reverse psychology does work - one such example would be at **Seaside Residences** in District 15. Those who are familiar with the district will know that freehold developments rule the estate - hence when Seaside Residences was launched in 2017, there were investors who scorned the idea of it being a 99-year leasehold development. The average PSF of the initial launch phase was around

$1,4xx - $15xx PSF (sounds dirt cheap by today's standards I know); back then you could get a less-than-5-year-old freehold unit in the resale market at the same price range in District 15, so it could be understandable why there would be buyers

Fast-forward to 2022, the average resale PSF went up as high as over $21xx PSF to $23xx PSF on average...

SOLD ON	ADDRESS	UNIT AREA (SQFT)	SALE PRICE (S$ PSF)	BOUGHT ON	PURCHASE PRICE (S$ PSF)	PROFIT (S$)
30 AUG 2022	12 SIGLAP LINK #XX-11	1,087	2,190	20 APR 2017	1,481	769,800
11 JUN 2021	16 SIGLAP LINK #XX-19	1,485	1,996	22 APR 2017	1,573	628,600
10 FEB 2021	18 SIGLAP LINK #XX-35	1,679	2,203	22 APR 2017	1,831	625,000
13 AUG 2021	10 SIGLAP LINK #XX-01	1,130	2,168	24 JUL 2017	1,711	516,000
10 DEC 2021	10 SIGLAP LINK #XX-01	1,130	2,122	14 MAY 2017	1,668	513,000
5 JAN 2022	10 SIGLAP LINK #XX-03	829	2,329	22 APR 2017	1,731	495,490
17 MAR 2021	10 SIGLAP LINK #XX-06	786	2,186	22 APR 2017	1,586	471,590
24 SEP 2021	10 SIGLAP LINK #XX-01	1,130	1,963	14 APR 2018	1,575	438,888
3 DEC 2021	12 SIGLAP LINK #XX-07	786	2,250	20 APR 2017	1,695	436,190
20 MAY 2021	12 SIGLAP LINK #XX-09	1,259	2,118	22 APR 2017	1,774	433,600
6 JUL 2022	10 SIGLAP LINK #XX-03	829	2,129	29 APR 2017	1,618	424,000
11 JUN 2021	10 SIGLAP LINK #XX-01	1,130	2,106	1 JUN 2017	1,732	422,000
17 JUN 2022	12 SIGLAP LINK #XX-11	1,087	2,097	23 APR 2017	1,718	412,000
15 FEB 2022	12 SIGLAP LINK #XX-07	786	2,163	22 APR 2017	1,646	406,400
27 JUL 2021	10 SIGLAP LINK #XX-04	764	2,262	22 APR 2017	1,741	398,328
15 JUL 2021	18 SIGLAP LINK #XX-35	1,206	1,891	1 OCT 2017	1,571	386,000
14 MAY 2021	10 SIGLAP LINK #XX-01	1,130	2,017	23 APR 2017	1,678	383,000
29 APR 2021	12 SIGLAP LINK #XX-15	1,206	1,924	22 AUG 2017	1,624	362,000
31 MAY 2021	18 SIGLAP LINK #XX-27	786	2,278	22 APR 2017	1,842	342,620
19 MAY 2022	12 SIGLAP LINK #XX-15	1,206	1,924	16 MAR 2018	1,642	340,000

Source: EdgeProp, URA

In just a matter of 4 to 5 years, Seaside Residences yielded high 6-figure profits (as high as $769,800!) for many property investors. Not bad for a 99-year leasehold surrounded by freehold properties isn't it?

The success of Seaside Residences can be attributed to 2 simple factors: **1. Excellent Product** and **2. Significantly Lower PSF Than Nearby Freehold New Launches**. While resale freehold properties in District 15 were selling at around $15xx PSF back then, freehold new launches such as Amber 45 were launched at $23xx - $25xx PSF on average - that's around $800+ PSF higher than Seaside Residences! With such a healthy margin to fall back on, the high profits were almost guaranteed.

In the meantime, those who bought the resale freehold properties in District 15 at $15xx PSF are probably still not seeing much profits... (Oops!)

Buy Freehold Surrounded By 99-year Leasehold

To be fair, even though this sounds like a no-brainer, it is extremely rare and difficult to find the right freehold product in estates that are heavily dominated by 99-year leasehold properties. As I had mentioned in Secret #18, there are many entry-level freehold developments in mass market areas, which you already know by now that it's a no-no to invest in those. The challenge would be to find a freehold project with high organic demand, without being significantly overpriced compared to the nearby leasehold counterparts.

Meanwhile, in prime districts such as District 9, 10, 11 and 15, you would find more freehold properties than 99-year leasehold properties... So where do we find a good freehold property that is surrounded mostly by leasehold developments?

One such development would be **Oasis Garden**, a freehold condominium in Bartley estate. Completed in 2009, it is a high-rise residential development that attracts organic demand not just because it's freehold, but also because it is located within 1 kilometre of Maris Stella High Primary (a hot favourite among many parents to send their boys to), and until recently, it was also the only freehold development with full condominium facilities among a cluster of 99-year Leasehold developments such as Bartley Ridge, Bartley Residences, and Botanique At Bartley.

SOLD ON	ADDRESS	UNIT AREA (SQFT)	SALE PRICE (S$ PSF)	BOUGHT ON	PURCHASE PRICE (S$ PSF)	PROFIT (S$)
18 SEP 2022	53 JALAN BUNGA RAMPAI #XX-06	2,350	1,417	16 MAR 2010	873	1,300,000
1 JUL 2022	51 JALAN BUNGA RAMPAI #XX-02	2,271	1,378	20 AUG 2010	960	950,000
6 JAN 2022	53 JALAN BUNGA RAMPAI #XX-06	1,335	1,483	7 JUL 2009	814	893,000
21 MAR 2022	53 JALAN BUNGA RAMPAI #XX-05	1,475	1,346	1 NOV 2007	889	674,700
6 NOV 2020	55 JALAN BUNGA RAMPAI #XX-08	1,216	1,254	25 MAR 2009	700	673,000
25 MAY 2018	55 JALAN BUNGA RAMPAI #XX-07	1,238	1,196	29 APR 2009	668	653,000
25 OCT 2019	51 JALAN BUNGA RAMPAI #XX-02	1,227	1,263	23 JUN 2009	738	645,000
31 JUL 2013	51 JALAN BUNGA RAMPAI #XX-02	1,227	1,263	17 JUN 2009	742	639,000
7 APR 2020	55 JALAN BUNGA RAMPAI #XX-07	1,238	1,284	26 JUN 2009	771	635,000
25 JAN 2013	51 JALAN BUNGA RAMPAI #XX-02	1,227	1,214	9 JAN 2009	700	631,000
28 JUN 2012	51 JALAN BUNGA RAMPAI #XX-02	1,227	1,149	5 JUN 2009	711	538,000
10 JUL 2013	53 JALAN BUNGA RAMPAI #XX-06	1,335	1,161	24 JUN 2009	769	523,000
23 APR 2013	51 JALAN BUNGA RAMPAI #XX-01	947	1,246	9 JAN 2009	700	517,000
24 JUL 2012	55 JALAN BUNGA RAMPAI #XX-07	1,442	984	14 MAY 2009	642	493,500
29 APR 2019	51 JALAN BUNGA RAMPAI #XX-03	1,227	1,296	31 JUL 2008	914	468,000
23 JAN 2013	55 JALAN BUNGA RAMPAI #XX-09	1,033	1,181	5 MAY 2009	745	450,000
20 MAR 2013	53 JALAN BUNGA RAMPAI #XX-06	1,572	1,012	4 AUG 2009	728	445,640
14 AUG 2019	51 JALAN BUNGA RAMPAI #XX-02	1,227	1,182	28 SEP 2007	822	441,000
26 NOV 2012	53 JALAN BUNGA RAMPAI #XX-05	1,475	1,139	22 NOV 2010	860	412,000
18 JUL 2012	55 JALAN BUNGA RAMPAI #XX-09	1,033	1,142	13 MAR 2009	743	412,000

Source: EdgeProp, URA

The highest profit at Oasis Garden? A whooping $1.3 Million earned by one of the owners of a 2,350 sq ft unit. It may have taken the owner 12 years to realise the 7-figure profit, but it is still a very notable result nonetheless. In the chart above, I've also highlighted transactions that yielded the owners healthy profits between $412,000 to $639,000 within just 3 to 4 years from the date of purchase. This proves that even if you're a short-term investor, you can also invest in a freehold development if you are able to identify the suitable ones that are surrounded by 99-year leasehold.

So... Where could we possibly identify more of such upcoming freehold projects?

Well, you might want to keep an eye out on future freehold developments along the **Greater Southern Waterfront (GSW)**. 6 times the size of Marina Bay, Singapore's government is going to develop plenty of new housing in this area - and every single one of the new developments in GSW will be a 99-year leasehold property, since they would be built on government-owned state land that would be sold to private developers through the Government Land Sales (GLS) tender.

That makes it extremely lucrative if you could secure a freehold unit before any of the GSW residential projects is announced, so I would suggest that you pay extra attention to the en-bloc collective sales of old freehold developments near GSW, especially in estates such as Pasir Panjang. With that being said, I certainly don't think there will be many new freehold projects available around GSW - so you might have to grab whatever you can get and pray hard that you don't miss out on the opportunities when they arise... It could just be the perfect chance for you to use the Reverse Psychology method to generate your own high 6-figure and even 7-figure profits!

CHAPTER 7

YOU AIN'T SUCCESSFUL TILL YOU SELL

Knowing when to buy and what to buy is only half the equation.

Selling is the final key to realizing your profits...

Secret #25 - To Hold Or Not To Hold... That's The Question

Ahhh... The ultimate crossroad that most property sellers face.

"Should I hold on for a bit more?"

"Is it a good time to sell now? Or maybe I should hold, since the price is going up?"

"If I sell, there goes my passive income from the rental..."

These are just some of the common questions that I've heard from property sellers. The dilemma of whether to sell or not, and if it's even a good time to sell at all. Instead of convincing them that they need to sell, I would often ask them back: "why do you even want to sell?"

Funny thing is, they usually don't expect a realtor to question their motives to sell. Shouldn't a realtor be convincing them that they should sell NOW and sell ASAP? Well, that's not the way I work. To me, if you do not have a strong compelling reason why you should sell the property, then don't sell. Everything starts from the sellers' motive - if you're not a highly-motivated seller, I wouldn't want to work with you. Why is that so?

Because a seller who doesn't even know why they are selling would end up wasting everybody's time. Not just my time, but also theirs, and any prospective buyers' time too. In my early days as a realtor, I've met sellers who pull out of deals at the last minute for many varying reasons. Some even decided not to sell at all after wasting more than 2 months of house viewings done. That's when I understood one thing - they weren't entirely sure about selling to begin with.

When I ask sellers why they would want to sell, they would start to reason out their intentions. Some intend to upgrade, some want to downgrade, some just want to sell while the market is hot so that they can cash out some money, and the list goes on. I would write down every reason that they've stated and repeat it back to them, so that they can hear for themselves what their true intentions are. I believe that repetition helps with confirmation - I want to confirm that they are keen and serious about selling their property, so that we don't end up wasting each other's precious time.

After confirming their intentions, I would then proceed to ask: "So what's next after selling? Describe to me what you would be looking to buy next... Because what you intend to buy next will determine if it is a good time to sell your current property now. If you do not have clarity on what's next, then don't sell."

What do I mean by "clarity on what's next"?

Simply put, you need to know exactly what you intend to buy, what price it is at, then figure out how we can finance the deal and manage the timeline between selling and buying.

Most people take a long time to sell their place not because it is a challenging unit to sell - it's because they are unable to commit to selling when there are no concrete plans for their next purchase. They would spend months (and even years) "shopping" around for an ideal property, and that would delay the selling of their property infinitely till the day their purchase is confirmed. Once they have secured the next house, selling becomes so much faster and easier.

"But maybe we shouldn't sell yet, the price might still go up some more?"

Well, even if the price does go up some more, it is also likely that whatever you are buying next will also become more expensive, so that's kind of back to square one. Also, if you've invested in stocks or cryptocurrency before (just as I did), then experience would tell you that it is often dangerous to wait for a higher peak to sell; the price could fall fast anytime and you could possibly have to sell for even less profits than what you could have gotten in the first place.

Although for real estate, prices don't fall as hard and fast as with stocks and cryptocurrency, it would also take a much longer time for the price to bounce back up significantly. That's why I would always advise my sellers to **set a targeted selling price for a certain profit margin based on recent transacted prices & expected valuation price.**

It is of course my job to sell for the highest price possible, and in some cases we can still definitely sell above market valuation. However, we are living in a generation where data is increasingly more transparent than before where every buyer can easily find out the recent transacted prices and valuations, hence that limits the sellers' bargaining powers when it comes to price negotiation.

The biggest issue of all would be the bank's valuation of your property. In Singapore, all private property buyers who require housing loans from the banks are subjected to a maximum of 75% loan (as at time of printing) based on the bank's valuation, not based on the agreed selling price. For instance, if the agreed selling price is $2 million but the bank valuation is only at $1.8 million at the maximum, then the loan would be 75% of $1.8 million only. Not only is the property overpriced by $200,000, the buyer would also have to fork out $50,000 more up front in either cash or CPF to make up for the shortfall due to the loan being capped by the bank valuation.

The only time when valuation doesn't matter is when the buyer is willing to pay in full cash to buy your property; in such cases there is no need to obtain any valuation report for the sale of the house. However, such cases are rare, and usually happens mostly in high-end prime districts where buyers are willing to overpay the odds for a rare, premium residential unit.

So the key to selling efficiently is to simply not be greedy. Everyone wants more money for sure (and obviously if I can sell the house for a higher price, I also earn more commission), but TIME is also money. What you wouldn't want is for your house to become the "white elephant" in the market - the one that everyone knows it's overpriced while the buyers go for other cheaper units, leaving your unit on the shelf for many months. Eventually, you would still have to lower your selling price anyway, and in the process you may have wasted several months of your time.

An experienced realtor who is well versed with the market movement would know how to study the market and accurately advise you the ideal selling price for your place. These days, realtors rely on real-time data sources to determine the fair selling price of any residential property, so it would be wise to save your precious time by relying on the expertise of a reputable realtor.

Go to **https://realestatesecrets.sg/apply** to get a private consultation with me if you would like me to help advise you on the sale of your property.

Secret #26 - Want To Sell With More Profits? STOP Doing This

"The more realtors I engage, the more exposure my property gets... Why should I stick with only 1 property agent?"

Ahhhh. The classic line that I've heard so many times from property owners. This is possibly one of the most common myths that is still a widespread belief till this day (and probably forever). Is it really true that having more property agents to market your property is better than having just one?

Unfortunately, the ugly truth is this: having more realtors to market your property DOES NOT help to increase more eyeballs to your property listing! Yes, you heard me right. In fact, what it does is to turn some potential buyers away, causing them to avoid your listing at all costs.

Let's think this through for a bit - assuming that over a single weekend, there are a total of 5 property buyers who happen to be interested in buying a property around your listing's location. Having more realtors does not magically increase the number of interested buyers - even if you have 10, 20 or more realtors, the number of interested buyers during that very weekend would still be just 5.

These 5 buyers would then do the very same thing - search for listings on property portals, shortlist listings based on how attractive they are (be it based on pictures or the asking price or both), then contact the agent directly to arrange for a viewing. If there are more than 1 agent marketing the same unit, most buyers would then try to test the agents and see who can get the cheapest selling price for them... And that doesn't bode well to you as a seller.

"Well, I'm sure every property agent has their own network of buyers... So having more agents is good for me, no?"

That is unfortunately also a myth. While there are property agents who do serve buyers, most agents who serve resale sellers do not actually have ready buyers on hand. When realtors tell you that they have ready buyers looking for properties in your area, most of the time they are just lying so that they can get to sell your listing.

Sometimes, even if your asking price is way too high, these realtors may still tell you that they will do their best to help you to fetch the price you want... Yet, several months later your listing would still be stuck on the market, while in the meantime these realtors may have already made some money elsewhere by making use of your listing. Wait, how is that possible?

Thanks to online property portals such as PropertyGuru, realtors are able to use your listing to attract direct buyers who are not being served by any other agents. That's where they can "swing" the buyers to other property listings after viewing yours (and most of the time the buyers would agree that your listing is overpriced) - and these buyers would end up buying another unit but not yours.

By having multiple agents to market your property, not only does it encourage these realtors to "make use" of your listing to swing buyers elsewhere (since you have no exclusive loyalty to them, they also don't have to remain loyal to you), it also devalues your property as buyers may assume that your unit is a tough one to sell (to them that's why you need so many agents to market the property).

In my early days as a realtor, I once encountered a HDB unit for sale in Woodlands. It was known as an "open-listing", which means there are multiple property agents marketing the unit with no exclusive agreement signed. To my horror, there were a total of more than 20 agents advertising for the owner!

Out of curiosity, I asked the owner: "since your property is an open listing, does it mean that you would pay the commission to any agent who manages to sell your house by bringing in a ready buyer?" and the owner replied "yes".

"Isn't it odd that you are paying commission to someone who is representing the opposite party? I mean... wouldn't the agent help his or her client to negotiate for a lower selling price than what you're asking for?"

The owner remained silent for a while, before replying this to me:"I can simply not choose to sell to them, until they meet the price I want."

While that sounds logical, the truth is that this seller does not have any agent who is genuinely acting in his best interests. I was certain that the majority of the agents just wanted to make use of this listing to swing their buyers elsewhere. Although I was a relatively new realtor back then, my instincts told me that he was not the right home owner that I would want to serve. I decided to walk away instead of asking him for the advertising rights to market his property.

Eventually, his HDB flat remained on the market for another 2 months before the house was sold for a much lower price than what was being advertised. I pondered to myself back then - what if he chose to go with only 1 exclusive agent to sell his house?

With an exclusive agent who knows how to qualify buyers, what you will get is less wasting of your precious time - you wouldn't want to spend week after week showing your house to buyers who are either not ready or even unable to afford your property. Furthermore, instead of having to deal with viewing requests (often duplicated) from multiple property agents, now you only have to deal with just 1 realtor who should manage the viewing appointments nicely for you, so that it takes up minimal time on your end (therefore less disruption for your schedule).

Having an exclusive agent also means that you have a realtor who can completely act in your best interests - he or she will be the only person who is in full control of the entire negotiation process with every single interested buyer, which also represents more leverage to get the best possible offer for your property.

If you want to sell your property for higher profits, then stop engaging multiple agents to market your property... It could do you more harm than good.

With that being said, while there are more than 30,000 realtors in Singapore, not every single realtor is able to help you achieve your desired results. There will be many who may come knock on your door or send you flyers every single week, but it doesn't mean that they are the right ones to deliver the results you want. Sadly, a lot of them may lie and deceive you in your face, only to end up wasting your time and even cause you to sell for much less than what you could have fetched.

Turn over to the next page to uncover the truth about these hidden lies that realtors don't want you to know.

Secret #27 - The Hidden Lies That Realtors Don't Tell You

Unfortunately, there are always black sheeps in any industry, and in real estate it is no different. While there are definitely ethical realtors out there who are genuine, honest, and wouldn't over-promise, there are also those who use gimmicks and lies to earn big commissions.

This is especially so when it comes to agents who offer their services to help you sell your property. What I'm about to share with you in this Secret will help you to avoid engaging the unethical realtors, as well as those who over-promise but under-deliver.

Why am I doing this?

Frankly, I'm sick and tired of seeing some realtors lie their way to success. I believe there are ethical ways to earn our money, and I certainly do not agree with some of the methods used by these black sheeps of the industry. Instead of relying on their real skill and craft, they resort to lies just to entice you to engage them... In my eyes, that's totally not cool. Perhaps I might become a public enemy among realtors as more consumers learn about these lies that I'm about to expose very soon here - but that's okay with me, if that means you don't fall into the traps laid by the unethical agents.

"Get More Exposure For Your Listing Through A Home-Tour Video!"

Made popular by none other than Property Lim Brothers, property home-tour videos are often used as a marketing gimmick by realtors to entice sellers. Realtors would tell you that they could either offer you the home-tour video for free, or even charge you higher commission than usual to have the home-tour video done.

Although it is not impossible to attract buyers via a home-tour video, the real truth is this: home-tour videos are used by realtors to attract more SELLERS instead of buyers! Yes, you heard me right. These home-tour videos are often used as part of these realtors' portfolio to showcase their "expertise", so as to entice sellers to engage their services. However, in reality there are hardly any buyers who would enquire directly through the home-tour videos to request for viewing appointments.

Besides, home-tour videos are so common nowadays, it's almost as if every single listing requires a video to be done before it can be sold. The harsh truth is that realtors don't really need a video to help you sell your house - with well-taken photographs that are professionally edited, as well as a virtual 360° home tour, it should already be sufficient to attract buyers (unless the unit is seriously overpriced).

Unless your realtor has a super large following on his or her social media accounts (thereby increasing the probability of reaching out to a potential buyer), the home-tour video is unlikely to attract many viewers' attention.

Perhaps you can take it that the home-tour video is more like a keepsake for you, as a way to remember fondly how your property was like before it gets sold to the next owner. Otherwise, the next time a realtor offers to do a property home-tour video for you, just know that it really doesn't add much value to the sale of your property.

"I Can Get Direct Discounts From Developers For You"

Another gimmick used by realtors, particularly for cases whereby the seller is looking to buy a new launch development after selling away the existing property. I've heard of many instances whereby the seller decided to engage a certain property agent, just because the agent promised that they can get more discounts from the developer than other agents.

Having worked with many developers myself, I can vouch that this is absolutely NONSENSE.

The truth is this - regardless of which agency the realtor may be from, the developer offers the same discounted price to any realtor. Some realtors will claim that they have a special working relationship with the developers, which again is a typical lie. There are usually just 2 ways to get discounts from developers - one is if there is already an existing promotional discount, and usually the selling price would already be nett; the other way is if the developer has a secret buffer for extra discounts (sometimes another 1%-2%), as they would have anticipated that there would be buyers who want more discounts to sweeten the deal further.

If it was 2016 and earlier, it would be true that certain developers were willing to entertain large discounts in order to sell the units that were left unsold. I recall that I once helped my buyer to get a 9.1% discount of more than $400,000 for a prime property in Bugis, and that was in 2016... In those days, such huge discounts were possible because there was less transparency with transaction data.

Yet with the increased data transparency today, developers are more wary and would prefer not to entertain impromptu requests for more discounts. What they want is to protect the caveats lodged for every of the sold units - it wouldn't reflect well on the developers if buyers discovered through transaction records that another buyer purchased a similar unit to theirs for a much lower price just a few days apart; it would inevitably open a can of worms whereby more buyers would want to get the same discount (or even more).

As such, developers today are more resistant towards buyers' requests for further discounts. There would then be agents who would offer you "kickbacks" - a form of rebate that comes from their commission earned from the developers. If any agent offers you that, RUN!!!

In case you are not aware, kickbacks are illegal, as realtors are not permitted by law to entice clients in engaging their services through offering rebates as a benefit. Furthermore, any undeclared rebate would also contravene laws set by Monetary Authority of Singapore (MAS), as the property loan for the purchase is supposed to be reduced due to the rebate; clearly most buyers do not declare such rebates, which means that they are literally also cheating MAS.

As such arrangements are illegal, you would also not be able to pursue any legal action against the realtor if he or she decides to go back on their word and not offer you the rebate as promised. There is nothing you can do if the realtor doesn't fulfill their end of the promise!

My advice to you is to not let greed get the better of you. Although it is not wrong to save some money with your property purchase, what is more important is to have a realtor who truly cares about your long-term benefits by helping you to identify the right development, the most suitable unit for you, and devise a feasible strategy that you can confidently execute when it's time to rent or sell the property.

"I Can Help You To Sell For Much Less Commission Than What The Other Agent Is Charging You"

This is the classic "under-cutting" agent. Even though it is enticing that you are able to save a few thousands dollars by hiring a realtor who charges you lower, let's take a step back and think through this rationally.

If a realtor comes up to you and says that they are able to charge you less, are they capable agents or are they the ones struggling to make ends meet, thereby their desperation to get any deals by any means?

If they are struggling agents, does it make sense for you to hire someone like that to market your property?

Furthermore, are these realtors portraying a positive energy or negative energy? This is important especially when it comes to the negotiation process with potential buyers. While the realtor might be hungry to close the deal, you probably would not want to have a realtor who reeks of desperation and ends up bursting the deal because of their over-eagerness that spooked buyers.

The true value of a realtor isn't about the home-tour videos, virtual tours, nor even the home-staging that they offer you when pitching to be engaged as your selling agent. Any realtor can offer you such "services", but what separates top realtors from the rest would be these two things: **prospective buyers management & negotiation skills.**

An experienced or well-coached realtor would know how to manage prospective buyers - this goes down to even the little details such as the pacing of the viewing appointments, managing buyers' expectations on the price, following-up with buyers to maintain their interest, as well as to position your property favourably compared to nearby competitors on the market. An often overlooked process is to qualify the buyers - not just in terms of affordability, but also in terms of personality and the potential ease (or difficulties) dealing with the buyer. The last thing you want is to deal with a demanding and calculative buyer, who makes the whole selling process a mentally straining one for you.

Subsequently when there is a serious buyer putting in an offer, that's where the negotiation skills of the realtor come into play. This is the most crucial part of any property sale, as the negotiation process would determine how much you would get from selling the house. Hiring top realtors could easily help you earn an additional 5-figure difference for your sales proceeds, so it would be worthwhile to pay a higher commission to gain more profits from your property sale.

So the next time you meet a realtor who offers to charge you less commission, think carefully if it is truly worthwhile to go with a realtor who doesn't have what it takes to charge you more.

CHAPTER 8
YOUR MULTI-MILLION LEGACY BEGINS

It is no longer a dream to leave behind millions for your next generation.

With the right real estate investments, it can be done in a systematic manner that operates like clockwork.

Take the bold step forward to leave behind a lasting legacy...

Secret #28 - Your Decision Today Determines Your Children's Future

If you're a parent, then I am certain that the future of your child / children does matter to you. As we all know, the cost of living would only increase - will your next generation be able to afford a comfortable and stress-free lifestyle, or will they struggle to make ends meet? It is indeed hard to imagine how much it would cost to own their own homes in the future...

Thankfully, through real estate investments, you can secure your children's future by leaving behind a valuable asset in the form of a private property.

In my time as a realtor, I've met many parents who decided to invest in properties using their children's names, which we know as "buying under trust". To buy under trust, there are several criteria to be met - the property must be fully paid for in cash, and as at time of print there is also a 35% Additional Buyer's Stamp Duty (ABSD) that has to be paid up front first, before being reimbursed within a few months' time after IRAS have checked through that the trust deeds are done properly to ensure the child / children remain as the rightful beneficiary of the property without any special conditions attached.

The function of buying under trust remains as an integral component to how wealthy families pass on their wealth to their future generations. So how does it work?

Let's assume that today you decided to purchase a $1.5 million property under your newborn baby's name, of which the child will gain full rights to the property after turning 21 years old.

By the time your child turns 21, the property value is likely to have appreciated further - it could possibly be worth over $2 million or more by then. As you had to purchase the property in full cash, there are no loan interests nor CPF accrued interests to worry about - the only expenses would be the monthly maintenance fees and property taxes, which can be easily covered by renting out the property.

So let's pretend that the monthly maintenance fees would be $350 and the property would be rented out for $4,500 a month consistently for 20 years.

The annual property tax based on the rates as at time of print would be $6,060 ($505 per month).

$4,500 monthly rent - $350 maintenance fees - $505 property tax = $3,645 gross rental profit per month

$3,645 x 12 = $43,740 gross rental income per year
$43,740 x 20 years = $874,800

So on top of the capital appreciation, you would have accumulated $874,800 just from the gross rental income alone in that 20 years... It's not hard to see how this $1.5 million property could easily generate an extra million dollars for your child in that 20 years' time. That's how the ultra-rich generate more wealth for their families by investing in real estate - they leverage on the asset to accumulate wealth on auto-pilot mode. This effectively helps to hedge against inflation and ease any worries about higher costs of living in the future. This way, your children would also be able to pursue a life of their own choice without having to go through the stress and struggles in an increasingly expensive world to live in.

"But... I don't have that much money now to invest in a property with full cash..."

If that's what you are thinking, it's okay. While you may not be able to afford to do so right now, it doesn't mean that you cannot do so forever (unless you are really cash-strapped now and cannot even invest in any private property)... Or at the very least, you can educate your children to start investing in a private property as soon as they can, so that they are able to be the ones leaving behind a legacy for future generations.

By investing in a private property, you can kick start the process of wealth accumulation. How fast you can grow your wealth will depend on your current age, income and affordability... The earlier you start investing, the easier it gets for you to acquire the wealth needed to buy a property under your child's name - what you want is to have time on your side. No matter how rich and wealthy you are, you cannot defeat time...

Therefore, leveraging on real estate could be the way to make your money work harder for you, and accumulate the wealth needed for your next generation and beyond.

Of course, if you do not have a high income, nor do you have enough cash savings too to begin with, then it would be impossible for you to participate in the "money games" that the rich play. Leaving a lasting legacy behind through real estate is one of those money games - and if you play it right, you can even enjoy an early retirement with millions in your bank account.

Let's jump to the next Secret where I'll share with you how you can do so for yourself.

Secret #29 - Your Million-Dollar Retirement Blueprint

Being a millionaire isn't such a far-fetch dream anymore.

Currently, 7.5% of Singapore's population have obtained millionaire status with personal net worth (not assets worth) above $1 million, and the country is already ranked 5th richest in the world. According to a report by HSBC, Singapore could even overtake China and USA for millionaires per population by year 2030, with an estimated 13.4% of Singapore's population being millionaires by then.

Are you feeling puzzled how this is possible? How could you also become a millionaire (if you're yet to be one now), and retire comfortably with more than a million dollars in your bank?

That's exactly what I'm about to share with you - a blueprint for your million-dollar retirement dream.

Before I go on, I need to put it upfront to you that this blueprint is only possible if you can financially afford to invest in a private property to begin with. I am not a magician; I cannot grow your wealth for you if you do not even meet the minimum requirements to start investing. This is the harsh reality of the world - cash is king, and the rich will always be in a better position to become richer. Those with affordability issues will always be facing an uphill struggle to catch up with the rising costs of living, and that will always remain true regardless of which generation we live in. It can only get more expensive from here, that's a fact.

So how much do you need to invest in a private property?

If you're reading this in 2022 / 2023, as of now I would say that a total of $400,000 in Cash and CPF savings would be ideal. Anything less would represent much less options for you, and most of these options are not going to be investment-worthy. And this entry barrier will only get higher eventually, as the price of private properties would only go up and not down.

10 years ago, you could possibly purchase a brand new 1 bedroom condo for only $600,000. Today, it would cost you around $1.2 million on average to get a similar brand new 1 bedder. It does send chills down my spine to think about how much it would cost to invest in another 10 years' time...

This is why I decided to come up with a retirement blueprint, be it for myself or for my clients. Without this blueprint, it would be insane to imagine how ordinary Singaporeans can afford to retire. Unless you're already a millionaire by now, I am certain that this blueprint can help you greatly.

"But... Why do I need a million dollars to retire? I am an easily contented person, living a simple life doesn't need a million dollars, no?"

If that's what you are thinking, then let me show you how much you really need for your retirement:

Assuming that you decide to retire at the age of 65, and you continue to live on for at least another 20 years after.

Estimated monthly expenses: $3,000
$3,000 x 20 years = $720,000

I believe by the time you're 65, $3,000 a month is only going to help you get by with a basic standard of living. We are not talking about enjoying a lavish lifestyle, no travelling around the world, no indulging in luxury of any sorts. Yet in 20 years it would already cost you $720,000.

So even with a million dollars, minus away $720,000 you would be left with $280,000. That only represents an additional $14,000 per year for the 20 year timespan - you have only $14,000 extra per year to enjoy a little more in life. It's not exactly a lot of money if you factor in inflation and the rising costs of living; I strongly doubt that an additional $14,000 a year would make a huge difference in our life by the time we're going to retire.

My million-dollar retirement blueprint isn't a plan to get you rich - it was devised to help you meet the basic requirements for a worry-free retirement. Of course, you can also possibly gain more than a million dollars if you follow my blueprint, but I do not want to over-promise you anything. My focus is in helping you to grow your wealth as much as possible so that you can enjoy your retirement, and hopefully even leave a legacy behind for your next generation. Nobody can predict what will happen in the future, but one thing is certain - by doing nothing, you will gain nothing.

So let's take massive action today.

The Million-Dollar Retirement Blueprint

If you recall what I shared with you in Secret #14, smart investors leverage on loans to invest in properties. As such, you do not pay 100% of the property price. Based on the current loan structure as at time of print, we are able to loan up to a maximum 75% of the property purchase price. That means we only need to fork up 25% of our own cash and CPF savings, along with the Buyer Stamp Duty.

That's how I came up with the concept of what I call **"DP Wealth"**. DP stands for Down-Payment - since with every property purchase, we only need to fork out the down-payment and the rest will be covered by loan, effectively we are using just the DP to accumulate our wealth.

DP = 25% of purchase price + Buyer Stamp Duty (4% of purchase price - $15,400)
Shortcut formula = Purchase Price x 29% - $15,400

No matter what the purchase price is, the DP formula remains the same.

To further illustrate the concept, I'm going to use a very basic and simple example here. Let's pretend that we are going to start off with a $1.5 million investment property that is a 2 bedroom at 700 sq ft in size.

$1.5 million x 29% - $15,400 = $419,600

DP Wealth needed = $419,600

This amount of $419,600 is effectively your "start-up capital", and the aim is to grow this figure into more than a million dollars as soon as possible through real estate investments.

Let's assume that this unit would appreciate by $300 PSF, that makes it $210,000 in profit. Now add that to your original capital of $419,600 and you would have approximately $629,600 of DP Wealth after selling your first private property.

Without having to fork out any additional cash (and provided that you meet the necessary loan eligibility), based on $629,600 you would be able to buy a property worth $2.22 million. Now let's assume that we invest in a 3 bedroom worth $2.22 million next, and it appreciates by $250,000 this time round (which is a very conservative figure - I've seen 3 bedders appreciate up to more than $400,000 but let's play down the numbers here).

Add that $250,000 profit to your DP Wealth accumulation, and now you have $879,600. You're now getting real close to the million dollar mark... Probably just 1 more property away. So with $879,600 you would then be able to go for a $3.086 million property for your third property purchase.

With an appreciation of just another $250,000 more, you would have in total $1,129,600 of DP wealth accumulated, which is after 3 rounds of property investment that would likely take up 12 to 15 years of your time on average. In case if you haven't realised, along the way I have not included any additional cash to invest in the 2nd and 3rd property - only the initial start-up capital of $419,600 was used, so you could continue to set aside your own cash savings during the entire time frame as an additional source of reserve cash.

Let's say this entire investment plan took you 15 years to realise the $1.1 million of DP Wealth accumulated. During the same time frame, you may want to put aside some money to invest in trusts and bonds that can give you a stable 5% return per annum (which is fairly safe to achieve) - let's say you put aside $12,000 per year (that's $1,000 per month) - in 15 years, you would be able to cash out more than $280,000 as your investment returns, thanks to the power of compounded interest.

Add this to your DP wealth, and you now have more than $1.4 million in cash savings after 15 years and 3 rounds of property investments.

By now you might be thinking... "How can it be so simple? I thought it would be more difficult than that!"

Well, the above example is a very BASIC and SIMPLE version of what my million dollar blueprint is like, using purely capital appreciation to roll the profits and accumulate wealth along with each round of property investment. If we go into a more complex model that involves rental income, and even buying more than 1 property each for couples, it becomes easier and faster to achieve your million dollar goal - you may even grow your wealth by many more millions!

The real difficulty of executing this blueprint isn't about the concept - after all, accumulating wealth through multiple rounds of capital appreciation is a straight-forward idea that is easily understood by all. The most integral factor that determines the success of this blueprint is essentially the identification of the right property to invest in - if any of the properties turn out to be a poor investment with significantly less profit (or even none), then the whole blueprint goes up in smoke.

The following image is a screenshot of an actual blueprint draft that I did for one of my clients. In 2020 they bought their first ever investment property (Florence Residences) through me, and as of today they are sitting on healthy paper gains of more than $300,000 (could be $400,000 but once again I'm being conservative here) and they are eagerly waiting to move on to the next step of their blueprint.

Age 31 2020 : Purchase 1st property ⇒ DP = $280k.
                    ↳ Under 99-1 tenancy in common

Age 34 2023 ⇒ Option 1 : Sell Florence, Buy 2 properties → Resale 3BR,
I own stay   Investment 1/2 BR.
I passive income +   Option 2: Hold Florence, part-share
capital appreciation.   CJ buys 2nd property → Depends on cash & CPF savings

            Florence target profit = $200k.
            Total DP Wealth : $480k. ⇒ Max property purchase price $1.7 mil

Age 40 2027-2029 : Option 1: Sell 2 properties, buy 2 or 3.
                              ↳ $200k profit each = $400k.
                              Total DP Wealth = $880k.

Age 50 2030-2039 : Flexible options → DP Wealth in excess of $1 mil (Max purchase price
                              ↳ • Continue to flip & invest   of $3.5m - $4m)
                                • Upgrade to better locations/size/view
                                • Upgrade to Landed Property.

                    ↳ Downgrade/Downsize. Fully paid property.
                      Excess CPF Wealth can be withdrawn after
                      age 55 for early retirement.

Note that my estimated profits for them for the 1st property was only $200,000 - which is now proven to be a very conservative estimate. They purchased a 2 bedroom unit with an unblocked landed view for less than $1.05 million, and today the unit can easily fetch $1.4 million or more.

As such, we are confident that the next step of the blueprint would not be an issue to achieve - this couple is now well-placed to own a 2nd property even without having to sell the first. Furthermore, as the profits turned out to be much higher than expected, they would likely be able to achieve their million dollar goal a lot sooner than forecasted. The next step is for me to identify for them what to invest in next that would generate at least $200,000 to $300,000 in profit, and help them to accumulate their million dollar retirement savings.

Given that they are still in their early thirties now, time is certainly on their side. The heavy responsibilities now fall on me to ensure that we remain on track with the blueprint, and that's exactly what I love to do most.

If you want me to help you with a personalized retirement blueprint, go to the following link to apply for a private strategy session with me, during which I will deep-dive into the most suitable long-term strategy planning for your real estate needs. Simply submit an application via the link below; my team and I will assess to see if you qualify.

Https://realestatesecrets.sg/apply

CHAPTER 9

THE FINAL ADVICE FOR YOU, THE NEXT TOP INVESTOR

Congratulations, you made it to this final chapter!

But this isn't the end; it's a new beginning for you.

Now that you're equipped with all the essential real estate investment knowledge, the last 2 Secrets I have to share with you in this chapter would be the most important of them all, if you want to be among the top real estate investors in Singapore.

It's time for you to step up to claim the life you really want.

Secret #30 - Top Investors Focus On This More Than R.O.I

Return Of Investment aka R.O.I.

I'm sure this term is nothing new to you. Pretty much every investor knows what R.O.I is, and for decades it has been one of the most relied on metrics to measure the success of an investment. Some even talk about R.O.E which is the Return of Equity, a more accurate measure if you are not paying for a property in full cash.

But none of these would be more important than what is known as C.O.I...

C.O.I stands for COST OF INACTION.

This is a term that I first learnt from my esteemed mentor, Dan Lok. He taught me how top investors in the world are focusing more on C.O.I now, and why it is less preferred to focus on R.O.I or even R.O.E.

If you think about it, there is no way to know what is the R.O.I of any investment until you have actually invested in your money and waited for the results to show. Any form of estimation and "expected R.O.I" is literally just an estimation. Nothing has happened yet, and the outcome cannot be guaranteed, no matter how we analyse data to justify our investment choices. What data does is to guide us on the probability of success, which to a certain extent still remains reliable for investors to depend on, but that's all to it. No investment advisor will tell you that you are guaranteed a certain profit (unless you're investing in something like fixed deposits).

C.O.I on the other hand is very real. It is the cost that you would incur if you do not take any action at all, and this cost can come in many different forms. It may be opportunity cost, or actual financial costs (can be 5-figure or even 6-figure) that you may incur. For instance, if you hesitated on a purchase, you could possibly end up paying even more subsequently for a less desirable unit after missing out on your initial top choice. Or it could be that you weren't confident to invest in the property market, only to realise later that you misjudged the situation and missed out on all the good opportunities while property prices have moved on and it is so much harder for you to afford any property now. How much has that cost you?

For some, C.O.I turned out to be extremely expensive for them, painful even.

One such true story was encountered by one of my associates, whose client wanted to sell his HDB Executive Maisonette (EM) unit. The client bought the EM at $580,000 in the 1990s, and the property is presently valued at $750,000. Sounds like a profitable property, yes? Along the years, they had many opportunities to sell at a profit and move on to a private property, but the owners hesitated and did not take any action, until only recently did they decide to sell off the flat to help their son to finance his own property purchase.

Unfortunately for the owners, despite having fully paid off their HDB loan, they had to refund back $1.05 million of CPF funds into their Ordinary Accounts if they were to sell the house. It would be a negative sale even if they sold the house at the "profitable" market valuation of $750,000, with $300,000 of CPF Funds that would be forfeited. As what I shared in Secret #13, this happens commonly among many HDB dwellers who are unaware of the dangers with their CPF accrued interests incurred on their HDB flat - the shortfall amount would be written off as if it never existed, but it's still hard-earned money that should have rightfully been there for retirement savings. These $300,000 could have been there for their retirement funds, but now it's as good as vanishing into thin air with no way to get the money back.

If the owners of this EM unit sold their property way earlier, not only would they incur a lower loss (or even possibly even see profits if they didn't fully pay off their property using CPF funds), they would have been able to also upgrade to a private property earlier at a much lower price than what it would cost today. Not only did they miss out on many opportunities to upgrade and re-invest during the last 20 over years, they are also holding on to a ticking time-bomb. In just another 5 years' from now, the total CPF refund required upon sale of the property would compound to more than $1.2 million... Scary isn't it? That's how compounding interest works.

And as it's a negative sale now with zero cash proceeds, they also do not have enough money to help their son with his property purchase. Talk about a lose-lose situation.

If you are thinking of buying a property today, I would urge you to not just focus on the R.O.I - instead, ask yourself this simple question: "what would happen if you choose not to buy today?"

Would it become less affordable to own a property in the future?
Highly possible, as property prices are unlikely to decline by a lot. Moreover, the older you are the higher the monthly loan installments would be, which may be a huge deterrent by the time you finally decide to invest years later. By not taking action sooner, you would likely have to pay more next time if you were to enter the market at a later time.

Would the government implement more cooling measures that would affect your affordability to invest?
Needless to say, this is extremely possible. Since 2009, there were a total of 15 rounds of cooling measures implemented, and every measure directly impacted the affordability of property buyers to cool down the market. It has become a norm for cooling measures to happen whenever property prices go up at a faster rate.

While some think that cooling measures represent an opportunity to invest when prices drop, most are deterred from buying at all because they could no longer afford to buy, which means missing out on huge opportunities. Unless you're a cash-rich buyer who is intending to pay for the property in full cash, your buying capacity would most certainly be impacted when further cooling measures are implemented.

If you currently own a property, is it better to hold on to it, or should you restructure your portfolio and look at other alternative properties that provide a better return? If so, what are the opportunities in the market?
Frankly, if your property is generating positive cash flow for you through rental income while still enjoying capital appreciation, generally I do not think there is a need to sell the property (unless due to personal circumstances; that would make an exception). However, it is essential to know if your property is still a valuable asset, or is it already a liability to you unknowingly.

Do a simple "health check" for your property at least once a year - look at your CPF statements and check for your total CPF funds used along with the accrued interests incurred, along with your outstanding housing loan balance that is yet to be paid off. Then check for an indicative valuation of your current property price either through a banker or a realtor - your property's sales should fully cover the outstanding loan and also the total CPF refunds with a healthy excess as your cash proceeds. If the numbers show that you would be facing a negative sale (or if it's likely to happen within the near future), then it would be wise to dispose of the property that is becoming a liability to you.

What I do for my clients is to conduct such "property health checks", and to also analyse the recent price movements and overall pricing trend to determine if their property is still worth holding on, or if it's better to sell it off and restructure the portfolio with another property that can provide higher returns. By doing so, I'm helping my clients to unlock the potential for them to generate more wealth instead of holding on to a property that is no longer a valuable asset.

Top investors know that C.O.I impacts them way more than R.O.I, because the potential costs of not taking action is real. It is not fabricated numbers that are speculative, but actual real numbers that you are dealing with right here and now. During my tenure as a realtor, I've come across too many people who suffered because of C.O.I - most of them were unwilling to take the step forward for their property investment plans because of fear, uncertainty, and lack of belief in what they can achieve. If you had read through all of the 30 Secrets that I've shared with you thus far in this book, you should be feeling much more confident in taking action with your real estate investment now.

Still unable to push yourself forward to do it?

Then I have just one last Secret to share with you to help you with that. See you on the next page.

Secret #31 - The Art Of Taking Action For Real

Have you ever wondered why there are so many people in this world, yet so few are living a successful life with complete financial freedom?

The reason is simple - the majority of the world's population are afraid of taking action.

It is scary for them to think about moving forward, and most of them resist change. That is due to a scarcity mindset, where they focus more on the negatives in life than to embrace positive thoughts. Most of the time, we tend to allow our thoughts to drift towards bad consequences or negative outcomes, and that isn't healthy.

How can you take action if you are constantly paralysed by fears and negative thoughts?

Today, I want to help you to overcome that. I want you to be able to think for yourself, for your loved ones, and to push yourself forward to go for the amazing life you've always wanted to live. Nothing can stop you except your own mind, you know this is true. All the noises you hear in your head are well, your own voices in your own head. And you know what? You can control what you choose to tell yourself.

In this final Secret of this book, I shall end off with 3 major tips that will help you to finally take the step forward towards the wealth and happiness you want. I've been very blessed to come across mentors who helped me along the way, and these 3 tips that I've learnt from them not only helped me to achieve the wealth I desired for, it also changed my life forever... So likewise, I wish that what I'm imparting you here will also help you in one way or another, no matter how big or small.

Tip 1: Identity Shift VS Mindset Shift

More often than not, we often hear how we should "shift our mindset", so that we can experience change and improve for the better. Although that is certainly true and valid, most people tend to fall back to their old ways even though they had "shifted" their mindset. The mindset shift is usually temporary; it doesn't seem to last...

The reason why their mindset shift wasn't sustainable is because they didn't shift their Identity.

By holding on to your old identity, it doesn't matter how much you attempt to shift your mindset. It's just like changing new clothes without changing who you are within - you're still the same person deep inside even though you appear to be different from the outside!

Identity shift represents a stronger transformation within you - you take on a new identity in life that you truly resonate with, as it is literally how you see yourself. Your self-perception and self-image is more powerful (and also potentially more destructive) than any mindset change - you cannot outgrow who you think you are.

For instance, if you have an identity of being a heavy smoker, quitting smoking is going to be challenging and difficult because you are still holding on to the identity of being a smoker. Yet if you speak to a non-smoker, that person will have no issues avoiding cigarettes completely because he or she does not even identify themselves as a smoker at all!

The human mind, for all its complexities in its construct, is actually rather easy to trick and re-program. Our actions are the by-product of our thoughts, so the way you think literally translates into what you end up doing. If that is so, then the wonderful news is that you can start off by proclaiming the identity you want to become! You can practise doing so by frequently using the words "I AM..." followed by what you identify yourself with. Do this every morning when you wake up, when you're on the way to work, whenever you see yourself in the mirror, before you go to sleep... Do it as often as you want, and the more you do it, the better.

If you want to be a successful real estate investor, just tell yourself "I AM a successful real estate investor".

If you want to be a great parent to your child / children, just tell yourself "I AM a great parent to my kids!"

If you aspire to be a better speaker, then tell yourself "I AM an amazing speaker, and my audience loves what I have to share!"

While this may sound too simple to be true, just recall back to the days when you were a child. Have you ever imagined yourself to be a superhero or a famous fictional character? Most of us once took on the identity of being Superman, Batman, Spider-man, Sailormoon, Snow White and so on... Perhaps you've even worn a superhero or a Disney's character costume before too. I am a huge Batman fan, and I recall wearing a Batman costume that my father bought for me from Movie World in Gold Coast, Australia when I was 8 years old. I loved wearing the costume, especially the Batman mask. In those moments when I wore the mask, I simply took on the identity of being Batman... I WAS BATMAN!

Well, at least in my mind I was. And I had so much fun being Batman! I played with all my Batman toys, imagining the storylines of my own which involved Joker, Robin, the Batmobile...

As a child, our imagination was our favourite playground. We could imagine anything we wanted, and we loved to role-play. You could be a doctor today, a police tomorrow, a fireman the day after. In every role we attempted to play, we assumed the role completely and convinced ourselves that we could be anything we wanted to be.

Now that we are adults, the power of imagination that we used to have is hardly put to great use anymore. Maybe for a long time you've forgotten how it used to be, but I hope you are now reminded how great your imagination and visualisation once were. Tap into the memory bank in your brain, and you will almost instantly remember how you did your own role-plays as a child... It wasn't difficult to change your identity back then, and it would be just as easy to change your identity today.

So ask yourself - what identity do you want to assume today to change the life you are living now?

"I think, therefore I am." - Rene Descartes

Tip 2: Imagine & Visualise Your Desired Outcome

Now that you have understood the identity shift, the next step would be to think about the desired outcome you want.

What kind of life do you imagine yourself to live in the next few years? Think about happy thoughts. Think about the beautiful places you would visit with your loved ones... Who will be with you in those wonderful moments? What car would you be driving in, what house would you be staying in?

Huge disclaimer though - I don't advise you to imagine something that's too far-fetched for you to achieve within a short period of time (such as thinking you'll strike it rich and become a multi-millionaire or even billionaire overnight, that you're going to upgrade from a HDB flat or mass market condominium to a Good Class Bungalow within the next one or two years). It isn't that it's impossible - there are indeed overnight millionaires and also very successful businessmen acquiring Good Class Bungalows even before turning 30 years old (Secret Lab chairs, anyone?)... It is that the challenge is on you to sustain that imagination, and SEE THROUGH IT until it gets done.

And it will be challenging to sustain your desire if it's a very very far-fetched dream that you want to turn into reality. There is a higher probability of disappointment, disbelief, and despair, especially when you keep believing that it will happen and yet nothing changes even after a few years. That's when your inner voice will say "See, I told you that it's impossible!", convincing you to stop believing in your imagination. Unfortunately, most people fail to sustain their lofty dreams and aspirations for long enough to see it come true, and that is not what I want for you.

What matters more is your PROGRESS along the way. You can start by setting mini-goals and multiple milestones that lead up to the main objective you want to achieve, so that you can live the life you want.

Example:
Main objective - lose weight by 5 kilograms in less than 20 days.

Mini goals

- *Exercise for 1 hour daily*
- *Avoid carbs (completely if possible)*
- *Reduce sugar intake (or none at all)*
- *Eat more fresh vegetables, less meat*
- *Drink plenty of water*

The above is exactly what I did for myself, and I achieved my objective in just 10 days! I am someone who never used to like eating fresh vegetables (salads were a big no-no for me), but after shifting my identity and visualising the outcome I wanted, I started to LOVE eating salads and greens. In fact, nowadays I would feel uneasy if I haven't been eating fresh greens for days. Talk about a real change!

Mini goals work like a checklist - you set achievable targets for yourself, and then you just do it. It is pretty much inevitable to achieve your objective eventually, as long as you complete the mini-goals necessary. Then PROGRESS will happen, and after achieving your desired outcome you can now set a new, bigger objective next.

That's how we keep improving, that's how we grow. Keep doing this and you will slowly witness your life being transformed for the better.

One of my mentors, Kelvin Fong once taught me: "It's not about Perfection, it's always about Progression", and this quote woke me up. I used to be a perfectionist (maybe I still am, but much less so than before now), and I was often frustrated whenever things didn't go the way I wanted them to be. The disappointments and failures often resulted in me feeling disheartened, and I struggled to push myself forward. Thankfully, I had a wise mentor in Kelvin who reminded me to focus on Progression, not Perfection, and that helped to turn my life around for me to become who I am today.

It is possible for you too to achieve the dreams and goals that you imagined - just work on it step by step, and you will get there.

"Success is steady progress towards one's personal goals" - Jim Rohn

Tip 3: Give Yourself 5 Seconds, And Just Do It

Procrastination.

A word that most of us identify with. It might even be something that you feel attached to, as if it is a big part of who you are. It is a silent killer that can stop you from achieving your dreams and aspirations; even if you're aware of its existence you might even give in to it hopelessly.

But you know what? You can choose to get rid of it. Procrastination is like a viral disease - while it is destructive, it can be cured if you are willing to.

And the wonderful news is that all it takes to cure your procrastination is just 5 seconds.

This method is known as the "5 Second Rule", a theory founded by best-selling author Mel Robbins. In her book "The 5 Second Rule", she talks about how we can overcome procrastination by mastering the self-management technique of making decisions within just 5 seconds. Mel Robbins believes that human beings tend to procrastinate if they are given too much time to think (and I doubt anyone will disagree), so we have to start to condition our mind to decide and execute our thoughts faster before hesitation creeps in.

The next time you have a task on hand or an idea to execute (especially if it's something you have to do no matter how unwilling you are or how difficult it would be), countdown 5-4-3-2-1 and then just do it.

You'll be surprised how easy it would be, and the more often you do this, the more accustomed to the method your brain would be. That's how you can develop a new habit of taking action fast without much hesitation, thereby increasing your productivity and actually draining less of your energy. I don't know about you, but for me procrastination tends to make me feel more tired instead. Taking action makes me feel alive, and the more active I am the higher energy I would have!

So give this 5 Second Rule a go, and keep practising it until it becomes habitual for you. Sooner or later, you will certainly reap the rewards and benefits from doing so!

As the saying goes, "Time Is Money", and that is always true when it comes to real estate. Every day, there will be houses sold in the market. While you are hesitating, someone else is taking action. Sharp investors are fast decision-makers because they don't want to lose out on their top investment choices, nor be at the mercy of sellers or developers increasing their prices subsequently.

Of course, I don't mean you should decide to buy a property right away after just 5 seconds. As you have learnt through all 31 Secrets in my book by now, there are so many factors to consider before you proceed with your property investment. It is a lot to absorb and learn I know, so take your time and read through the Secrets again if need be to ensure that you understand completely how you can invest in Singapore's properties in a safe and systematic way for predictable gains.

Also, I have 2 additional Bonus Secrets that you can unlock online (if you haven't done so) - go to **https://realestatesecrets.sg/bonus** to complete the following Bonus Secrets:

- Secret #32 – "What's New, What's True In Real Estate Today" - Learn The Latest Property Market Trends And Spot Where The Next Gold Mine Will Be!
- Secret #33 - "3 Steps To Riches" - The Framework For A Fulfilling, Carefree Life That You've Always Wanted!

To acquire more real estate knowledge, you can also go to my online store at **https://ceekay.sg/store** to purchase my online digital courses, and you may also follow me on my social media handles:

TikTok - @ceekay.sg
Instagram - @ceekay.sg
YouTube - Ceekay Soh

So that's it, you've completed this book now, and in your hands you have the knowledge of more than 30 Secrets about investing in Singapore real estate. Although it is indeed a complex market to invest in, there are still many who successfully profited from their real estate investments, and you can also be one of them too. The Secrets you learnt from this book will serve as a guide to assist you in spotting the right opportunities in the market, so use what you learnt wisely.

Years down the road from now, there will always be people who would lament that they missed out on golden opportunities to invest in real estate… And I sincerely hope that you wouldn't be one of them.

Wish you all the best with your real estate investments, God Bless.

Printed in the USA
CPSIA information can be obtained
at www.ICGtesting.com
LVHW041451021224
798042LV00006B/195